ARM IN ARM

A R M

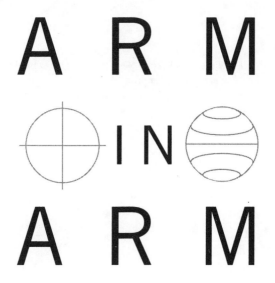

IN

A R M

THE POLITICAL
ECONOMY OF
THE GLOBAL
ARMS TRADE

William W. Keller

BasicBooks
A Division of HarperCollins*Publishers*

Table 5.1 reprinted courtesy of *Defense News*. Copyright © by Army Times Publishing Company, Springfield, Virginia.

Designed by Elliott Beard

Library of Congress Cataloging-in-Publication Data
Keller, William W. (William Walton), 1950–
    Arm in arm : the political economy of the global arms trade / William W. Keller.
        p.   cm.
    Includes bibliographical references and index.
    ISBN 0–465–02667–2
    1. Defense industries.   2. Arms transfers.   3. Arms race.   1. Title.
HD9743.A2K45   1995
338.4'76234—dc20   95–23152
                                                                            CIP

95 96 97 98 ❖ /HC 9 8 7 6 5 4 3 2 1

For Lonna

CONTENTS

CONTENTS

PREFACE

From 1989 through 1991 I directed a study of the global arms trade under the auspices of the U.S. Senate Armed Services Committee and the House Committee on Government Operations. In the course of that study, we conducted interviews at approximately one hundred arms firms in Western Europe, East Asia, and the United States.

I came away from this experience with grave concerns about a world-class problem: the global diffusion of the most powerful weapons and the technologies that underlie them. It is a problem that many people think has gone away. The end of the cold war has relieved their sense of urgency about regional arms races and the spread of technologies associated with conventional weapons and those of mass destruction. I found the opposite to be true: globalization of military industry and technology *accelerated* at the end of the cold war, it did not decrease.

This book examines developments that do not bode well for international peace and security. The first of these is the apparent support among governments for the transfer of potent weapons—advanced attack aircraft, submarines, tanks, missiles, munitions, radars, and the like—to the less developed world. A second trend is the formation of business alliances among arms manufacturers of different nations. In the 1990s, the transfer of military technology and the production of weapon systems is fast becoming a global enterprise. Third, advanced civil technology is increasingly being adapted to military purposes. A good example is the injection of high-technology commercial electronics into missile guidance systems, smart munitions, and other information-intensive weapons. And finally, technologies that support weapons of mass destruction are being acquired by more and more countries in the developing world.

I do not believe that the future is determined by technology. But we have reached a juncture in history at which technology poses a significant threat to the maintenance of a stable and peaceful international system of nation-states. Military technology is being developed and diffused rapidly, right along with commercial technology. This is happening at a time when distinctions between the two are breaking down. Moreover, the advanced industrial states appear determined to arm developing countries, even though those countries are increasingly able to absorb military technology and to augment it. The growing technological acumen of a range of developing nations is cause for concern because it applies not only to technologies associated with the arms industries, but also to those that underlie nuclear, biological, and chemical weapons.

In the absence of a clearly defined threat to their security, the developed nations of the West have relaxed cold war controls on dual-use technologies—technologies with both peaceful and military applications. In addition, there has been a fundamental shift in the rationale for exporting powerful conventional weapons. The national security justification has given way to an economic one: whereas arms exports once served to oppose Soviet power in the developing world, they are now necessary, at least according to their proponents in the United States, to provide jobs for Americans and to maintain the U.S. military-industrial base. I doubt this argument can be sustained, and have taken pains to debunk it in the pages that follow.

The pressing question is how to reconstruct the international system of states in the aftermath of the cold war. This is a task made more difficult by the widening distribution of increasingly powerful weapons of all kinds. It is the lesson of the Persian Gulf War and the massive arsenal that President Saddam Hussein of Iraq bought from foreign powers to pursue the war with Iran and his invasion of Kuwait. America led the charge and won the Persian Gulf War. But we have not yet fixed the fundamental directions of U.S. foreign policy or determined the underlying dimensions of international relations for the decade to come.

The post–cold war world is not a safe place. It is being made less safe by traffic in advanced weapons and militarily useful technologies. This can only exacerbate regional tensions unmasked by the end of Soviet suppression of ethnicity and religion and by the demise of U.S.-Soviet bipolar stability. Far from ushering in a new era of understanding among nations, the end of the cold war has unleashed the old potentials for regional conflict based on ethnic, tribal, religious, and national differences.

In this book I have tried to avoid some of the language typically used to describe military affairs. I have done so in order to widen the discourse, to bring in readers whose understanding can make a difference in the unfolding of events, but who have been excluded from the debate because it is excessively technical or because it is inconvenient to address their concerns and objections. If we can engage a broader audience, beyond a few government specialists and knowledgeable academics, then it is at least possible to shift the terms of the debate. To this end, I have narrowed the scope of some terms and expanded the range of others, two in particular.

The word *defense*, for example, is used extensively by governments and in the pertinent literatures as a euphemism for several more accurate words like *war*, *weapon*, *military*, and *arms*. The United States used to have a War Department; now it is a Department of Defense. We talk about defense systems, the defense industrial base, and defense technology, but what we really mean is weapon systems, arms industry, and military technology. Because language defines the discourse, the choice of terms can delimit or extend the dimensions of the problem. If all we are doing is selling defense equipment to improve the defensive capabilities of our friends and allies, who could quibble with that? But when we and our allies arm the world, friend and foe alike, that is another matter.

If the word *defense* is too big and indiscriminate, another term, *proliferation*, must be expanded and enriched. Proliferation typically refers to the spread and multiplication of nuclear, biological, and chemical weapons. But this limited usage excludes the spread and multiplication of advanced conventional weapons, strike aircraft, for example, which are now routinely sold throughout the world. Many of these aircraft were specifically designed to deliver nuclear, biological, and chemical ordnance. Their proliferation should be a matter of great concern. In this book, the concept of proliferation also extends to the advance and global diffusion of military industry and technology; it is the principal issue in the pages that follow.

William W. Keller
Weld, Maine

ACKNOWLEDGMENTS

In many respects, this book is the end result of a study I started in 1989 at the Office of Technology Assessment (OTA), an agency of the United States Congress. My colleagues at OTA contributed a great deal to my thinking about the arms trade, proliferation, and the global diffusion of military technology, both during the OTA study and over the past three years, when I was writing this book. Having said that, however, I must issue the standard disclaimer: The views expressed in this book are those of the author, and do not necessarily reflect those of the Office of Technology Assessment or the committees of Congress that requested the 1989–91 OTA study.

This book would not have been possible without the generous support of the Carnegie Corporation of New York and the Peace

ACKNOWLEDGMENTS

Studies Program of Cornell University. Judith Reppy at Cornell and Virginia Gamba of the MacArthur Foundation were of great assistance, especially in the research phase of the book, as was Malcolm DeBevoise of Princeton University Press, who suggested that I write it in the first place.

Theodore J. Lowi and William Greider both provided strategic insights and suggestions for revision toward the end of the project. Richard A. Bitzinger, Gerald L. Epstein, Allen Greenberg, Bruce W. Jentleson, Thomas H. Karas, Peter J. Katzenstein, Todd M. LaPorte, Lora Lumpe, Louis W. Pauly, Andrew J. Pierre, Simon Reich, David Rosenfeld, and Richard B. Samuels read one or more chapters at different stages of the work and made many helpful comments.

I owe the greatest debt for their time and talents to two colleagues in particular: Paul N. Doremus and Carol V. Evans. Each read the full manuscript, provoking me to further drafts, and generally clarifying the structure of the book and the content of the analysis. Like the institutions cited above, my friends and colleagues must also be held harmless; any errors or omissions are mine alone.

ARM IN ARM

1 APPROACH TO ARMAGEDDON

THE PARADOX

In the winter of 1991, President Saddam Hussein of Iraq learned an old paradox: that more weapons can lead to less security. The United States and the other major arms-producing nations are now in the process of learning the same hard lesson. Pursuit of domestic security through acquisition of powerful weapons is creating the conditions for instability and decreased international security on a global scale. The arms trade, and the steady diffusion of technologies that underpin weapons of mass destruction, lead not to more security and stability, but to less, and, in the end, to decreased autonomy for buyer and seller alike.

As the United States and its allies prepared to attack Iraqi forces and drive them from Kuwait, a number of contradictions and unpleasant realities emerged to dampen euphoria at the end of the cold war. First, the "new world order," trumpeted by the White House, would be initiated by a nasty war in the Middle East, one that threatened Western access to Persian Gulf oil and required deployment of nearly 540,000 troops.[1] While some commentators likened Saddam's conquest of Kuwait to Hitler's remilitarization of the Rhineland, no serious analyst envisioned conflict on a world scale or a significant military threat to the security of the West. Similarly, there was talk of "containing" Iraq, but that word had lost its ideological force and was oddly out of context. The chief concerns were that Israel would be drawn into the war, weakening the political base of the United Nations (UN) coalition, possible use of unconventional weapons, the disruption of oil supplies, and the residual effects of environmental warfare.

A second reality: few of the weapons comprising the vast arsenal through which Saddam hoped to prosecute his "mother of all battles" were produced in Iraq or even in the Middle East. Military industry in Iraq is primitive by Western standards. Saddam turned to outside powers. From 1981 through 1988, the period of the Iran-Iraq War, Iraq imported $61 billion in arms principally from the Soviet Union, France, China, and Germany, but also from Eastern European and several developing nations. During the same period, Iran bought $19 billion in military equipment for a combined total of $80 billion.[2] Because neither nation was capable of producing modern conventional weapons, the character of the Iran-Iraq War might have been quite different. If outside powers had refused to supply arms to the Persian Gulf, Saddam might not have invaded Kuwait, but even if he had, liberating Kuwait would not have required the largest and most powerful invading force since the Second World War.

More reality: Iraq was armed with chemical weapons and had demonstrated their use, both against the local Kurdish population and in the war with Iran. Nerve and blister agents were used effectively in the final campaign that defeated Iran in 1988.[3] Iraq also possessed Soviet-made Scud B ballistic missiles and had developed, with considerable foreign assistance, two indigenous variants, the Al-Husayn and the Al-Abbas.[4] Scud missiles, designed in the Soviet Union in the 1950s, are crude and inaccurate by today's standards, but can deliver both conventional high explosives and weapons of mass destruction. They can also be modified to increase range and payload. During the Persian Gulf War, Iraq attacked Israel and Saudi Arabia with ballistic missiles, armed with conventional warheads.

After the Persian Gulf War, when the United Nations inspectors went to catalog and destroy Iraq's weapons of mass destruction, they found thirty Scud missile warheads at a launch site, filled with nerve agents. Sixteen contained a mixture of GB (sarin) and GF.* According to one UN official, "The other 14 warheads were of a binary type. These were found with alcohol already in the warheads and with canisters of DF [a nerve agent precursor] at the sites for filling the warheads just before firing."[5] Perhaps Saddam chose not to use chemical warheads because he feared a nuclear response from Israel. Perhaps the intensity of the U.S.-led air assault, with more than 112,000 sorties in forty-three days, prevented their use.[6] Whatever the reasons, the spectacle of the entire Israeli population preparing for unprovoked chemical assault, sealing off rooms and putting on

---

*DF is a nerve agent precursor, methylphosphonic difluoride. Adding isopropyl alcohol to it makes GB (sarin); adding a different kind of alcohol to it makes GF, a related nerve agent.

3

gas masks, was broadcast around the world. The presence of chemical weapons in Iraq and nuclear weapons in Israel altered the character of the confrontation. As the world watched spellbound, a game of high-stakes roulette unfolded in which it was never certain, until the end, that chemical and even nuclear warfare could be averted in the developing world.

Western companies helped Iraq produce weapons of mass destruction. Over 130 German companies, including industrial giants such as Messerschmitt-Bölkow-Blohm GmbH (MBB) and Karl Zeiss, supplied unconventional weapons technology and chemical precursors to the Iraqi chemical weapons program.[7] The Karl Kolb firm was identified as a principal contractor for the large-scale nerve gas plant at Samara.[8] German firms also shipped "large quantities of stock materials and components needed in the manufacturing of gas centrifuges for the production of enriched uranium."[9] Although Iraq did not produce fissile material using this method, a small amount of enriched uranium was produced with calutrons using electromagnetic separation technologies.

Scores of German technicians worked in Iraqi missile laboratories and provided German technology to extend the range of the Scud B missiles.[10] Not long after the Iraqi missile attacks, Hans Dietrich Genscher, the German foreign minister, visited Mosha Erens, then Israel's minister of defense. At that meeting Erens handed Genscher a German fuel pump that had fallen from the sky during a Scud missile attack, and is reported to have said "I believe this belongs to you."[11]

Of course, German companies were not the only ones. American firms, perhaps unwittingly, assisted the Iraqi nuclear weapons program by selling nuclear technology and devices allegedly earmarked for Iraq's nascent nuclear power industry.[12] Such exports were, of course, subject to U.S. government controls, requiring an export license on a case-by-case basis. But the controls were ineffective. In reviewing the license applications, nuclear scientists at Los Alamos National Laboratory, where U.S. nuclear weapons are designed, discovered a pattern of exports clearly indicating that Iraq was developing a nuclear weapon. When they reported their discovery to higher authorities in Washington, they were overruled and the stream of exports continued to be approved.[13]

War with Iraq exposed many contradictions, and especially so for France. French weapons had been used effectively by third world nations against France's allies on at least two occasions: when Exocet missiles destroyed the British ship HMS *Sheffield* in the Falklands War, provoking public euphoria in Paris, and against the USS *Stark* in 1987.[14] But the Persian Gulf War marked the first time French forces expected to face modern French arms, including large numbers of Mirage F-1 fighter aircraft, Exocet and TOW (tube-launched, optically tracked, wire guided) missiles, and many other sophisticated weapons made in France and sold to Iraq. Moreover, the French air force could not operate its top-of-the-line Mirage fighters in the Persian Gulf War because they could not be distinguished from those flown by the enemy. Adding insult, about $5 billion worth of the weapons in Saddam's arsenal still belonged to France because the Iraqis were delinquent in their payments.

France was not alone in facing the realities and contradictions of a "new world order" that had, after all, inherited the implements and industries of war fashioned during forty years of bipolar superpower confrontation. Iraq's primary motivation in acquiring foreign military equipment in the 1980s was to fight and win the war with Iran. Indeed, following a string of decisive Iraqi victories in 1988, military imports to Iraq fell in 1989 to $1.9 billion from an annual average of $7 billion during the previous eight years of war.[15] Whether Saddam invaded Kuwait to obtain ports in the Persian Gulf, settle old scores with his neighbors, establish regional hegemony, or control world oil prices will continue to be matters of debate. But the existence of a million men under arms, equipped with the best weapons money could buy, dramatically raised the stakes—for Saddam, for the Iraqi people, for the Kurds, for Arab and Israeli alike, for the UN-authorized military coalition, and for the international community as a whole.

The paradox of international security is, as Saddam learned, that more arms can lead to less security; the acquisition and diffusion of increasingly powerful weapons both ensures and subverts the sovereignty of nations. In the end, even after victory at Al Faw and Kermanshah, the arms acquired failed to enhance the power and prestige of the Iraqi state.[16] Far from it. They ultimately caused the United States and its coalition partners to project massive force into Baghdad on a scale that would never have been contemplated, much less executed, in their absence.

From the French perspective, the paradox is several times removed, compared to the devastation of Iraq. Yet it is deeply embedded in French procurement policy because France relies on export revenues to sustain its arms industry.[17] As French officials explained several months prior to the Persian Gulf War, insufficient foreign demand could cause them to cancel major projects, for example, the Rafael fighter aircraft. At the same time, these officials identified the principal military threat to France not as the Soviet Union, but as unstable and irresponsible regimes in the Persian Gulf and North Africa—their clients.[18]

The advent of hostilities with Iraq exposed contradictions for the United States as well. As the cold war wound down, the world's remaining superpower engaged in what looked like a police action to secure its interests in the Persian Gulf. Was it, in part, an outgrowth of the failed policy of the 1970s, when the United States sold $11 billion in military hardware to the shah of Iran and trained eleven thousand Iranian military officers?[19] The weapons failed in their purpose, to enhance the stability of a friendly and moderate government in the region, and were later used to wage war against Iraq. As the Islamic revolution spread outward from Tehran, the arming of Iraq gained the logic of resistance, and although the United States did not sell weapons to Saddam, it did not protest but quietly encouraged French and other transfers.[20] That war, and the associated orgy of arms sales to the belligerents (and to other states in the region), lifted Saddam Hussein and raised the general level of armaments to dangerous, disproportionate, and ultimately unstable levels. Was the United States then compelled to step in to redress the imbalance?

Arms-exporting nations in both the advanced and developing worlds continued to provide weapons to Iraq even after the end of the Iran-Iraq War in 1988. They failed to identify Iraq and its well-equipped, massive army as a threat to the security of the Middle East and to global economic interests. One construction of events sees the arming of Iraq and the rest of the Middle East as an epiphenomenon of East-West confrontation, a kind of rough juggling and balancing of Soviet and U.S. clients. Another emphasizes the disparities of rich and poor states. Others seize on the Arab-Israeli dimension, or the historical basis for seething ethnic, tribal, religious, cultural, and nationalist hatreds. Still another focuses on an abundance of mature arms industries around the world, on largely unrestrained competition for lucrative Middle East arms markets. All of these perspectives are useful, but none is sufficient. Even as the Persian Gulf War revealed many contradictions, others were in the making; the principal arms exporters, who also happen to be the five permanent members of the United Nations Security Council, continued to transfer advanced weapons to the region—at record levels.

In different ways, Saddam, France, and the United States confronted aspects of the paradox of international security, but this paradox does not depend on regional animosities or ideological conflict, or even begin or end in the Middle East. It rests instead on a sequence of steps that starts with legitimate pursuit of security through acquisition of arms, and culminates in arming the enemy and in nuclear strategies of mutual assured destruction. It is deeply embedded in preparations for the cold war, the sharing of new weapons and technology within the North Atlantic Treaty Organization (NATO) and Warsaw Pact alliances, and the export of weapons to surrogates in the developing world. But that is less than half the story. What remains, in the aftermath of the cold war, is the steady diffusion of increasingly powerful military technology, and the construction of sophisticated centers of military industry around the globe. As East and West backed down from the brink of total nuclear confrontation, proliferation in all its forms—nuclear, conventional, chemical, dual-use, biological, and of military industry and technology itself—created the underlying conditions for an increasingly volatile and potentially hostile world.

THE THREAT

As politicians everywhere proclaimed the end to forty years of nuclear confrontation between East and West, a new threat emerged: the threat of sporadic militarism. To some it was embodied in the person of Saddam Hussein and the vast force he assembled to crush Kuwait and achieve his objectives in the Arab world. But Saddam did not spring full blown from the sands of the Syrian Desert. He was, instead, propped up by the profligate arms export policies of the advanced industrial democracies and the Soviet Union, and the inability of these states to contain the underlying technologies for weapons of mass destruction.

We have reached a threshold where even the most destructive and sophisticated weapons are available to an expanding range of political actors and industrial organizations. In the field of conventional armaments, the ability to acquire weapons is a direct consequence of the policies of the major arms-producing states: they have entered into active international collaboration in military technology among themselves, and have promoted the export of advanced weapons and the associated production technologies to the developing world. The increasing availability of these weapons is also tied, more and more directly, to the infusion of commercial technology into weapon systems, and the so-called civil-military integration initiatives, promoted by the Pentagon in the mid-1990s.(These initiatives are discussed in the second section of chapter 5.)

In this era of rising uncertainty and international chaos, we are stuck with the legacy of the cold war: not only political disintegration, but also the physical remains of four decades of technomilitary confrontation. The knowledge and industrial infrastructure built up during the cold war is increasingly available, extending incrementally to less developed nations. And it is not only military technology but the whole sweep of high-tech industries that is spinning on new materials and modes of information processing and storage, suitable for both commercial and military ends.

As national governments procure less military equipment, arms companies increasingly seek technological synergies and economies of scope and scale associated with multinational production for global markets. Facing overcapacity and exponential increases in the cost of developing new weapons, they seek, like other high-technology industries, to establish international networks of supply and production, and to export components and finished weapons to meet demand wherever it may exist.

Arms firms of different nations have entered into strategic alliances, joint ventures, licensed production and codevelopment activities, and many other business arrangements that transfer militarily useful technology from one country to another. As trade in military and dual-use technologies expands, both among the advanced industrial states and from them to the less developed world, new centers of military industry and technology have emerged around the globe. Each new center is capable of transferring technology and selling weapons to additional countries. The primary result is the globalization of military industry itself. The collateral effect is the gradual and collective loss of political control over potent weapons emanating from many parts of the world.

We have entered an era where global communication, industrial infrastructure, and multinational insertion of technology into the world economy is breaking down national and political boundaries, and with them the allegiance of corporations to nations. As the differences between military and civil technologies diminish, so too does the distinction between public and private control. Increasingly, companies, not nations, own and manage the crown jewels of the global military industrial enterprise.

The Persian Gulf War provided evidence that it is dangerous for the makers and sellers of arms to ignore the consequences of largely unrestrained global trade in modern weapons. In the ten years preceding that war, the value of global arms exports totaled $669.4 billion, of which $522.1 billion, or about 78 percent, were acquired by developing nations. In simple terms, the NATO and Warsaw Pact countries armed the developing world, exporting approximately 90 percent of the weapons.* After the cold war, the West continued to make massive sales of weapons to developing countries, even though it is undeniable that the presence of vast and increasingly sophisticated arsenals among likely belligerents raises the stakes associated with regional instability and conflict.

The tragedy is that the modern industrial nations and their former communist adversaries are fueling the breakdown of international security in both the advanced and developing worlds. Disintegration takes place on two distinct levels. First, advanced nations are the principal arms merchants of the world, and increasingly, they have also sold the means of production (the underlying manufacturing technologies) associated with combat aircraft, missile systems, tanks, radars, artillery, battleships. At a second level, they are the purveyors of nuclear, biological, and chemical technologies that are intended for peaceful purposes, but which can also be used to construct weapons of mass destruction.

Like most tragedies, this one involves a choice: with respect to conventional weapons at least, it is clearly possible, as a matter of public policy, to promote or to retard the globalization of advanced military industry and technology. For now, the modern industrial democracies have chosen to tolerate and even to support the global transfer of weapons and technology among themselves and to states and firms in the less developed world.

In 1995, for example, the United States issued an arms transfer policy that paid lip service to the idea of restraint, but, for the first time, also explicitly supported arms exports as a way to shore up U.S. military industrial interests. A principal goal of Presidential Directive 41

---

*Figures are calculated from Arms Control and Disarmament Agency (ACDA) data using 1993 constant dollars. See tables 3.4 and 3.6 in chapter 3 for specific citations.

was "to enhance the ability of the U.S. defense industrial base to meet U.S. defense requirements . . . at lower costs."[21] Moreover, U.S. officials were instructed to consider "the impact [of the sale] on U.S. industry and the defense industrial base" as a general criterion for decision making on U.S. arms exports.[22] The fact that the new policy contemplated arms exports as a way to support the U.S. arms industry was important: by the mid-1990s, the United States already accounted for 50 to 60 percent of worldwide arms exports, and was forecast to maintain or surpass that level to the year 2000 and beyond.[23]

With respect to nuclear, biological, and chemical weapons, there is a clear consensus, at least in the developed world, that such implements of war and their underlying technologies must be controlled. But the dual-use character of the technologies involved, and the international economies associated with them, militate against the ethic of restraint in the long term.

A policy that promotes extensive commerce in military technology and advanced weapons is shortsighted in the extreme. It treats the arms industry as though it is merely another sector of the international economy. It says that economic forces should determine the allocation of potent weapons, not political ones, and that foreign military sales should be used to bolster the military production base at home. This logic encourages the dissemination of dangerous conventional weapons of all kinds. Did the West defeat Soviet communism only to make the world safe for American and European weapons? Is this the meaning of the end of the cold war? Or does the removal of a potent adversary also imply the need to change policy, to delimit and circumscribe commerce in modern weapons and military technology in the interest of world peace and stability?

For individual states in the less developed world, the acquisition of sophisticated weapons may provide the illusion of invulnerability, but time and again, equivalent or superior weapons fall into the hands of an adversary, upsetting the military balance and upping the stakes. There are too many sources of supply to believe that the logic of conventional superiority can be sustained. At the same time, the high costs of acquiring, operating, and maintaining modern conventional forces may lead some states to seek weapons of mass destruction.

Leaders of small states who would acquire great weapons place their autonomy as well as their development at risk. Historically, they became clients, mere messengers and placeholders of the superpowers. In the emerging world order, they risk dependence on supplier states, both for training and maintenance of existing weapons and for financing and supply of new ones. More important, the acquisition of powerful weapons, both conventional and those of mass destruction, often causes an adversary to seek similar capabilities, feeding a bilateral or regional arms race. Finally, if small states deploy nuclear weapons or invade lesser nations, they risk intervention by the great powers, intervention that can destroy their armed forces, dismantle their nuclear, chemical, and biotechnology industries, and lead to sustained economic and political isolation.

For the modern industrial democracies, whose prosperity and weapons are backed by high technology, a rising level of armaments worldwide threatens the global system of trade and multinational production that has brought unprecedented wealth. As more developing nations buy or build powerful weapons, vital political and economic interests are placed at risk. At the same time, the military power of some developing states, and the fear of igniting regional conflict, constrains the options available to democratic leaders. Increasingly, belligerents in the Middle East, in Central Asia, on the Indian subcontinent, in the Balkans, and elsewhere are highly armed, and may even possess nuclear, biological, or chemical weapons.

This situation suggests the critical importance that global arms trade and commerce in technologies associated with weapons of mass destruction will exert on international and foreign affairs for the foreseeable future. If present policies and trends persist, they will produce a world in which the power and diffusion of modern weapons of all kinds continuously undermine relations among states, disrupting alliances and increasing uncertainty and risk in international relations. By exporting massive amounts of potent weapons and the associated production and delivery technology, the advanced industrial states continue to build up the ability of potentially renegade states or terrorist organizations to make trouble, to threaten the use of force, or to attack weaker neighbors. The Persian Gulf War and the breakup of Yugoslavia initiated the post–cold war order; if modern weaponry continues to proliferate at present rates, they may come to characterize it.

The collapse of Soviet power ended a relatively stable, if bipolar, system of alliances and assumptions that welded together diverse interests, cultures, and religions on both sides of the conflict. A far more complex and less coherent world is emerging, where ideology and military alliance are no longer the defining characteristics but lesser elements, and where the relative position of states is increasingly a function of their technological and economic development.

Those who would chart the course face a world in which weapons interact with a variety of political uncertainties. Principal among these are conflicts associated with the end of Soviet suppression of ethnicity in Eastern Europe and Central Asia, rising religious strife and nationalism on the Indian subcontinent and East Asia, and long-standing ethnic, religious, and tribal antagonisms in the Middle East and Africa.

According to the U.S. Central Intelligence Agency, it is also a world in which "a growing number of countries [more than twenty-five] are seeking advanced weapons, including nuclear, biological, and chemical weapons, as well as missiles to deliver them."[24] In the words of its counterpart organization, the Russian Foreign Intelligence Service: "proliferation of weapons of mass destruction constitutes a particular danger in this connection. It is spreading like the metastasis of a cancerous tumor, can strike the entire fabric of international relations, and undermine hopes for the creation of a just and stable world order."[25]

THE CHALLENGE

The challenge is to create international political institutions capable of controlling the allocation of weapons among competing nation-states, and failing that to consider a range of coercive measures that might be more unilateral in character. Such institutions and such measures would have to reflect the particular circumstances associated with different kinds of weapons and modes of proliferation. In the case of conventional weapons, for example, the right of states to provide for their own defense, and, by extension, to arm their allies is universally recognized.[26] But in the fulcrum of the cold war, this right was leveraged out of all proportion. Seeking more arms with greater lethality, accuracy, and sophistication became an end in itself. It has led to overcapacity in the arms industries, to the stimulation of regional arms races by overeager sellers, to fiscal crisis in the Soviet and American states, and of late to the increasingly multinational character of armaments research, development, production, sales, and service.

With respect to weapons of mass destruction, proliferation is the result of a complex of factors, but not to overt policies of the advanced

15

industrial or Soviet successor states, whose leaders have almost universally attempted to stem such proliferation per se. The relevant factors vary considerably, depending on whether the weapon is nuclear, biological, or chemical, its level of technical complexity, and the available means of delivery. There can, however, be little doubt that the dual-use character of many of the technologies underlying weapons of mass destruction increases the likelihood of proliferation. This problem is considered in chapter 2.

It may, nevertheless, be possible to circumscribe or delimit the right of nations to make, possess, and distribute weapons. Although arms control is in its infancy, weapons of mass destruction and missiles above a certain range and payload are increasingly subject to bilateral and multilateral restraints. In the field of conventional weapons, the Treaty on Conventional Forces in Europe (CFE) established numerical ceilings for tanks, personnel carriers, artillery, aircraft, and helicopters that could be deployed in Europe by the NATO Alliance and former Warsaw Pact members.[27] But no similar agreement reaches beyond Europe to the developing nations, where there are no restrictions on the conventional weapons that states can deploy, develop, or buy from outside powers. Policy makers have remained unable to grapple with the issue of what constitutes excessive production or trade in modern conventional weapons.

The trade in combat aircraft provides an apt illustration. First, it is manifestly impossible for any developing country to design and produce a modern fighter aircraft without significant outside assistance. Second, over the past two decades, the trade in such aircraft—including the F-16, F/A-18, F-15E, Mirage F-1C, Tornado IDF, SU-27, and MiG-23 among many others—has been vigorous, and production technology is increasingly included.[28] Acquisition of foreign military technology has enabled Turkey, India, China, South

Korea, and other nations to achieve local production of many different combat aircraft. Third, because of the arms transfer policies of the major arms-producing states, highly capable combat aircraft are widely dispersed around the globe. Many of these aircraft have ground attack capabilities, and could be modified to deliver weapons of mass destruction over a longer range and with greater accuracy than many missiles. Moreover, combat aircraft are the only weapon systems that have delivered nuclear weapons, and might well be the delivery vehicle of choice for a nuclear weapon originating in the developing world. This simple chain of logic is well known to policy makers in the West and in Russia, but it has not caused them to constrain the trade in military aircraft.

Responsible world leaders have, however, established international control regimes directed at the most destructive weapons and technologies. These include the Nuclear Nonproliferation Treaty (NPT), the START Treaties, the Missile Technology Control Regime (MTCR), the Nuclear Suppliers Group (the "London Club"), the Chemical Weapons Convention (CWC), the Australia Group, the Biological and Toxin Weapons Convention (BWC), and others. On its face, the list is impressive and suggests that much is being accomplished. But many of these measures are informal, lack enforcement provisions, or address only part of the problem.

If fully implemented, for example, the START I and II Treaties would reduce by half the number of deployed strategic nuclear weapons in the former Soviet Union and the United States. In the best case, where all nuclear weapons in Ukraine, Kazakhstan, and Belarus are consolidated in Russia, the START Treaties would still represent less than a 50 percent solution—because they are fundamentally bilateral. As such they do not affect the declared nuclear weapons states of France, the United Kingdom, and China, the undeclared or so-called "threshold" powers, Israel, India, and Pakistan, or a range of other proliferant nations that are thought to be seeking nuclear weapons: Iran, North Korea, Iraq (now in enforced reversal), and possibly Libya and Algeria.

The Missile Technology Control Regime is another important example. It is an agreement among twenty-two nations to limit the proliferation of missiles capable of delivering weapons of mass destruction, and to reduce or eliminate international transfers of associated components and technologies. Its overall purpose is to minimize the risks associated with the proliferation of nuclear, chemical, and biological weapons by controlling trade in delivery systems and their underlying technologies. But the status and requirements for states participating in the MTCR are nebulous in the extreme. As one noted authority observes, "there is no organization as such to join and no treaty or document which requires signature."[29] The Regime does not set limits on the kinds of missile technology that participating states can develop and deploy on their home territories.

In this and other aspects, the MTCR is flawed, both conceptually and administratively. First, it specifically excludes trade in manned aircraft, the most widespread and credible vehicles for delivering ordnance of all kinds.[30] Second, it was designed to permit trade in missiles that fall below specified range and payload limits, and to permit trade in antitactical ballistic missiles.[31] Third, with respect to administration, there are no multilateral enforcement provisions and no inspections, and governments are to implement the MTCR "in accordance with national legislation."

In the U.S. case, for example, "it is understood that the decision to transfer remains the sole and sovereign judgment of the United States Government."[32] In practice, the criteria used by the United

States to determine whether or not to export a given technology or component are flexible and a matter of continuous bureaucratic wrangling between the Departments of State, Commerce, and Defense.[33] As a result, the United States applies different criteria to different nations, and various member-states of the MTCR often disagree on what is in fact controlled by the Regime.

In its most elemental form, the challenge is to control the proliferation of powerful modern weapons. It involves an apparent trade-off between the autonomy of the nation-state and the structural integrity of the international system of states. The power of modern weapons suggests that both cannot be obtained. In a world with widely diffused weapons of all kinds, it will be necessary to compromise national autonomy to achieve a military balance among states and within regions at sustainable levels.

As will be shown in later chapters, this view is confirmed both by the history of proliferation and by the logic of deterrence. If we cannot establish universally binding and enforceable limits on the technologies and weapons states may acquire or export, then it is likely weapons of all kinds will continue to proliferate. The critical question is whether the increasing power and dispersion of modern weapons and the underlying technologies will outpace the evolution of international political institutions and norms required to regulate and control them. This is and will remain an open question for the foreseeable future.

2 PROLIFERATION

AFTER THE PERSIAN GULF WAR

In the wake of the Persian Gulf War, the United Nations Security Council established a Special Commission to locate, catalog, and destroy Iraq's weapons of mass destruction (WMD), its longer-range missiles and superguns, and the means of producing them. In the first six months of operation, the Commission (working in conjunction with the International Atomic Energy Agency [IAEA]) sent twenty teams to carry out on-site inspection of Iraqi nuclear, biological, and chemical weapons, and ballistic missile facilities.

That Iraq possessed chemical weapons was no secret. Both nerve and blister agents were widely reported to have been used in combat with Iran and internally to suppress an insurgent Kurdish minority. They were also well known to foreign governments because German companies, among others, had supplied and helped to construct the nerve and mustard gas facilities at the Muthanna State Establishment, a major complex of approximately 170 square kilometers, located near Samara. An early UN inspection report characterized conditions at Al Muthanna as "hazardous in the extreme," with chemical agents present in some areas and buildings. Most major structures at the facility had been destroyed or heavily damaged in the Persian Gulf War.[1] The Muthanna State Establishment was subsequently designated by the UN authorities as the central repository and site for the destruction of all chemical weapons found in Iraq.

At Muhammadiyat, a chemical weapons storage facility west of Baghdad, "leaking chemical munitions were scattered among thousands of unexploded conventional munitions, 122-millimeter rocket motors and other ordnance." The sixth UN chemical weapons team counted some "2,000 bombs and 6,200 artillery shells filled with mustard agent, as well as several thousand 122-millimeter missile warheads filled with the nerve agent sarin."[2] Six months after the UN Special Commission to disarm Iraq was set up, its executive chairman reported that it seemed "probable that a full assessment of Iraq's chemical weapons capabilities will be achieved." By that time, the inspectors had found and Iraq had acknowledged "46,000 filled chemical weapons munitions; 79,000 unfilled chemical weapons munitions; over 600 tons of chemical weapons agents; and some 3,000 tons of chemical precursors." In the area of biological weapons, the UN teams discovered a "major military research program in Salman Pak concentrating on anthrax and botulism."[3]

If the magnitude of Iraqi chemical weapons production surprised some observers, the international community was taken aback by the scale, sophistication, and maturity of the nuclear weapons program. On the basis of on-site inspections and Iraqi top-secret documents, the UN team concluded that "Iraq was engaged in a broad-based effort to design and develop an implosion-type nuclear weapon." The nuclear weapons program, code-named "Petrochemical Three (PC3)," was centered at Al Atheer, a facility specifically dedicated "to design and produce a nuclear device." The UN inspectors also determined that Iraq had three different (and parallel) uranium enrichment programs, that it had engaged in substantial international procurement of nuclear weapons–related equipment, and that the full extent of Iraq's nuclear weapons program might never be known. Iraqi officials confiscated documents, detained the UN inspectors, and generally obstructed the inspection process.[4] But perhaps most unsettling was the disclosure that within one year to eighteen months, Iraq might have produced an indigenous nuclear weapon.[5]

Most, if not all, foreign governments were unaware of the extent and maturity of the Iraqi nuclear weapons program, even though, as Bruce Jentleson has shown, the United States possessed ample intelligence of Iraqi intentions, but failed to act on them.[6] Iraq was a signatory to the NPT and a member of the IAEA, subject to IAEA safeguards. It was, nevertheless, able to conduct extensive uranium enrichment and weapons design efforts without detection. At a minimum, these revelations point to serious flaws both in the use and interpretation of military intelligence, and in the arms transfer policies of a variety of nations that supplied Iraq. Had they known, would France, the former Soviet Union, and China have continued to ship delivery vehicles to Iraq? Would German technicians have continued to work in Iraqi ballistic missile projects?

As successive inspection teams returned with increasingly fantastic findings, the magnitude of Iraq's ambitions began to affect the character of Security Council deliberations. When Iraq denied the existence of its nuclear weapons program and sought to obstruct the investigation, the Security Council responded with a tough mandate, Resolution 707, which reasserted the powers of the Special Commission to disarm Iraq and extended its tenure. The executive chairman of the Commission, Rolf Ekeus, characterized the Security Council actions as "a great breakthrough . . . a watershed." He stated: "For the first time now they recognize that the existence of weapons are a political manifestation. . . . You have to have control of the weapons in order to get security."[7]

The United Nations not only approved military intervention in Iraq, but in the aftermath, engaged in intrusive and coercive inspection and destruction of the arms of one of its own member-states. This unprecedented assumption of powers by an international body had far-reaching implications, not only for Iraq and other would-be rogue states, but also potentially for the UN as an institution itself. The decision to move against Saddam involved recognition on the part of the international community that there are conditions under which the acquisition of weapons cannot be tolerated. The subsequent decision to destroy Iraq's weapons of mass destruction set another precedent. But stark as this sounds, it is only a start.

MODES OF PROLIFERATION

Policy makers have failed to conceive of, much less address, the problem of proliferation in a comprehensive and dynamic way. Most of the discussion centers on nuclear, biological, and chemical weapons—the so-called weapons of mass destruction. In recent years, however, longer-range ballistic and cruise missiles have been added to the mix, because they are efficient vehicles for the delivery of nuclear, biological, and chemical weapons. At the same time, and in an apparent logical disjunction, shorter-range missiles, combat aircraft, and submarines— all of which can deliver weapons of mass destruction—continue to be traded widely, presumably because they are deemed to have legitimate roles in conventional warfare.

The technical hurdles, lethality, and delivery requirements of nuclear, chemical, and biological weapons are highly dissimilar. Nuclear weapons are harder to make or acquire than biological or chemical ones. But they do not need to be targeted as precisely, nor do they require means of dispersing submunitions or aerosol technologies associated with chemical and biological agents. Unlike biological weapons, nuclear bombs inflict catastrophic physical damage and can render large areas uninhabitable for many years, although biological weapons can be just as lethal when directed against population centers.[8]

Many chemical agents are bulky and harder to deliver than nuclear or biological weapons, easier to defend against, and unlikely to achieve comparable fatalities, even among urban populations. A recent nerve gas attack in the Tokyo subway, for example, resulted in only twelve deaths, even though the deadly chemical agent sarin was released in several sites during the morning rush hour.[9] Indeed, in some respects, chemical weapons may have more in common with conventional warheads than with other weapons of mass destruction. Both nuclear and biological weapons can be quite small and easy to deliver compared to chemical or high-explosive warheads. Under some circumstances, chemical weapons are easier to defend against than conventional bombs.

When direct comparisons are made, the neat distinctions begin to break down. In a concerted attack involving hundreds or thousands of sorties, for example, conventional weapons can achieve levels of devastation associated with the term *mass destruction*. Over fifty years ago, the firebombing of Tokyo and Dresden, which antedated the development of fuel-air explosives and napalm, produced physical destruction and casualties far exceeding those typical of most attack scenarios involving chemical weapons.[10]

Apparently, weapons can be placed in one category or another, depending on a range of factors. Nuclear and perhaps biological weapons may constitute a class apart. As a recent analysis of the technical aspects of proliferation has suggested, the agents used in biological weapons are "hundreds to thousands of times more potent than the most lethal chemical-warfare agents, making them true weapons of mass destruction with a potential for lethal mayhem that can exceed that of nuclear weapons."[11] There is, accordingly, far more to fear from the proliferation of biological and nuclear weapons than chemical ones.

Moreover, the relative ease of developing biological and toxin agents, the difficulty of detecting them, and the dual-use character and wide availability of the requisite technologies may even place biological weapons in a class of one. That is, many more nations could acquire or develop biological weapons than nuclear weapons, although biological agents do pose significant technical challenges in some forms of delivery. About a dozen countries are thought to possess or to be seeking biological and toxin weapons, despite the ban imposed by the Biological and Toxin Weapons Convention.

As the devastation of Tokyo and Dresden showed, conventional arms can be used for purposes of mass destruction. Similarly, it is possible to configure and employ nuclear, biological, and chemical weapons so that they do not inflict massive casualties. These observations and comparisons suggest that the category "weapons of mass destruction" is based as much on historical usage as on logical grounds or on analysis of the characteristics of various kinds of weapons. This has tended to legitimize arbitrary limits on nonproliferation, both intellectually and in terms of specific treaties and regimes. "Mass destruction" has so dominated our thinking about nonproliferation that we have ended up with the Nuclear Nonproliferation Treaty (NPT) for nuclear weapons, the Biological and Toxin Weapons Convention (BWC) for biological weapons, the Chemical Weapons Convention (CWC) for chemical weapons, the Missile Technology Control Regime (MTCR) for missiles, and very little else.

These regimes have rightly sought to codify controls on extremely dangerous weapons, but at the same time they have extended a measure of tacit approval to other forms of proliferation. If it is not a weapon of mass destruction (or a longer-range missile to carry one), then it is presumed to have a legitimate place among conventional armaments. As such, there should be few, if any, controls over which states may produce it, its legitimacy as a traded commodity, and whether or not the underlying production technologies may be transferred to additional countries. The choice is between a narrow and a broad definition of proliferation, and we have opted for the former.

In this context the MTCR, even with its many flaws, represents an important advance. Missiles are not weapons of mass destruction. But the addition of longer-range ballistic and cruise missiles to the list of weapons of proliferation concern extends the problem of proliferation into the field of conventional armaments. This is where a more dynamic concept of proliferation is needed to assess the spread of increasingly powerful weapons through several distinct modalities.

Proliferation is not merely the metastasis of nuclear, biological, and chemical weapons capability (and some missiles) to additional sights around the globe. It is a phenomenon that is both economy-wide, extending to the process of industrial and technological development itself, and, at the same time, embedded in the political economy of relations among nations. Table 2.1 suggests three broad elements of proliferation, which can be logically ordered but not divorced one from the others.

In the lexicon of international security, the term *proliferation* has typically been reserved for several classes of weapons (and the associated technologies) that are controlled or prohibited in international commerce. These are listed as the first two end-items in table 2.1: weapons of mass destruction and longer-range missiles. But shorter-range missiles are widely traded in the military aerospace sector, and many can be upgraded to increase range, payload, and accuracy.

The trade in combat aircraft, which is analyzed later in this chapter, also constitutes the principal means by which vehicles capable of delivering weapons of mass destruction are disseminated around the globe. Moreover, extensive commerce in the underlying manufacturing technologies makes indigenous assembly and production of many components of these aircraft possible for a range of developing countries. The distribution of these end-items is now seen, by military planners as a threat: that is, we must configure forces, build weapons, and take other steps to counter the military end-items distributed via export and the transfer of enabling production technology. The four groups of end-items in table 2.1 form a logically continuous whole, making increasingly advanced weaponry available to many nations and industrial organizations.

Firms and states both provide transmission belts for the diffusion of potent weapons, with the difference that firms are far more efficient. Both public and private sector structures or channels of proliferation form a second category in table 2.1. To achieve scale economies

TABLE 2.1. ELEMENTS OF PROLIFERATION

I. End-Items of Proliferation Concern

Weapons of mass destruction: The spread of nuclear, chemical, and biological weapons and associated enabling technologies.

Missiles: Limited to ballistic and cruise missiles above a specified range and payload that can deliver weapons of mass destruction, and to the associated technologies.

Global arms trade: International commerce in military goods and services, specifically including but not limited to a wide range of delivery vehicles suitable for WMDs (exclusive of longer-range ballistic and cruise missiles).

Commerce in military technology: The sale, license, or other means of transfer of military technology to a foreign government or company, often including production technology.

II. Structures/Channels of Proliferation

International collaboration: Joint development and production of military systems by arms companies of two or more nations—often involving exchange of technology, cost-sharing, and joint acquisition of the end-items.

Multinational arms business: Widespread application of multinational forms of business organization to the military industries, including strategic alliances, foreign direct investment, and intrafirm technology transfer.

Globalization of military industry and technology: The spread of new centers of military industry and technology throughout Europe and Asia and to the developing world.

III. Drivers/Dynamics of Proliferation

The export imperative: The need to achieve scale economies and access to foreign markets in order to afford the development and production of modern weapons—exacerbated by reduced military spending after the cold war.

Elimination of export controls: The effort to remove cold war controls on dual-use technologies (includes spread of dual-use technologies).

Economic development: Technologies and industries that underpin the advanced national economies—aerospace, nuclear power, chemicals, pharmaceuticals, biotechnology—also enable the development of weapons based on those technologies and industries.

associated with multinational production of complex weapons, arms companies of different nations establish strategic alliances, joint ventures, licensing arrangements, offset agreements, and other methods of sharing military technology and production processes. In the buyers' market of the 1990s, foreign customers increasingly demand significant technology transfer as a condition of the sale. They hope to achieve local manufacture of as much of the plane, tank, missile, or other weapon as possible. During the cold war, hundreds of major weapon systems entered into joint and licensed production among companies based in Europe, Asia, and North America. The cumulative result has been the widening distribution of military industry and technology on a global scale, with the corollary that firms, not nations, exert increasing control over the distribution of modern implements of war.

Such arrangements became increasingly common among the advanced industrial states in the 1970s, and were extended to Korea, India, Israel, and a large number of other developing nations in the 1980s. Over the past decade, many European and U.S. arms companies began the transition to international sourcing, production, marketing, and sales that American multinationals had pioneered in the commercial sector during the 1960s and 1970s. The result, over time, is the globalization of military technology and associated production infrastructures. New centers of military industry and technology have spread throughout Europe and Asia and into the developing world.[12] By the mid-1990s, arms industry representatives and Pentagon officials in Washington placed a high priority on achieving efficiency of procurement by drawing on the global arms industrial and military technology base.

After the cold war, the globalization of the arms industries was driven by a number of dynamics or processes of proliferation, the third category in table 2.1. Large-scale arms producers of many countries argued that, in addition to international production, they must also export fighter aircraft, for example, to help meet the escalating costs of developing new models for domestic consumption. As military acquisition budgets fell in the 1990s, and industry reconfigured to meet reduced domestic demand for weapons, arms exports became ever more important in the business plans of many U.S. arms companies.

But the imperative to export arms is only one among several factors driving proliferation. As the 1980s drew to a close, U.S.-based companies increasingly complained that national security restrictions on the export of many advanced technologies and products made U.S. industry less competitive than it otherwise would have been.[13] The inhibition against the export of a range of dual-purpose technologies was removed because it was no longer necessary to keep them from the Soviet Union. By the mid-1990s, companies whose international business prospects had long been hampered by U.S. export controls found themselves under increasing pressure from sophisticated competitors in Asia and Europe in a large number of high-technology industries. Some European and Asian firms were reluctant to do business with U.S. companies because of unpredictable delays in the U.S. export licensing process and requirements that they not transfer certain dual-use items to third parties.

In response, the Clinton administration stepped up efforts to eliminate unilateral national security barriers to the export of dual-use technologies and products such as computers and telecommunications equipment.[14] The Coordinating Committee for Multilateral Export Controls (CoCom) was formally disbanded in March 1994. But as of mid-1995, no new organization had emerged to take its place, in part because of American opposition to Russian contracts to sell MiG-29 and SU-24 fighter bombers, Kilo-class submarines, T-72 tanks, and other weapon systems to Iran.[15] In addition, it was difficult to reach agreement on lists of items to be controlled as well as to designate a list of proscribed recipient states.

In the late twentieth century, the distinction between military and civil technology is, itself, breaking down; the leading edge of many technologies now resides in the commercial sectors of the economy. Engineers are finding new ways to incorporate commercial developments into information intensive military systems. The Pentagon has undertaken a concerted effort to reduce barriers between the military and commercial sectors of the economy. These had built up during the cold war as a result of the comprehensive system of federal acquisition regulations and close oversight of the military contract sector by the Department of Defense, urged on by Congress. First in Asia, then in Europe, and now in North America, nations and firms have sought to take advantage of technological synergies by integrating civil and military research, development, and production.

Finally, the problem of proliferation intersects with fundamental processes of industrial and economic development. Sixty years ago no nation had the capacity to produce and deliver nuclear weapons, for example, or the firepower associated with modern conventional weapons; forty years from now it is possible that a great many nations will have both. The process by which countries achieve economic development is particularly implicated in the proliferation of the technologies and know-how that can result in the ability to acquire weapons of mass destruction and the conventional, yet sophisticated, means of delivering them.

In the broader context, it would be extremely difficult and equally undesirable to inhibit processes of technology acquisition and industrialization in the developing world, merely because we fear proliferation. For this reason, the NPT was designed to extend the benefits of nuclear power to those nations that would forgo nuclear weapons and agree to abide by a system of safeguards administered by the International Atomic Energy Agency (IAEA). In striking this bargain, the framers of the NPT assured that nuclear technology would become widespread, albeit for peaceful purposes, but it could never be withdrawn. There are now at least two signatories to the NPT, North Korea and Iraq, that have not honored the terms and conditions of the treaty. These exceptions notwithstanding, it may be that the effort to contain nuclear weapons proliferation and enhance the development of legitimate nuclear power will buy time. Perhaps not. (The question of the spread of nuclear weapons is addressed at the end of this chapter.)

COMBAT AIRCRAFT

The buildup of conventional forces in the developing world correlates with indigenous programs to acquire weapons of mass destruction. This linkage was evident in Iraq, but it is even more pronounced among the undeclared nuclear weapons states, India, Pakistan, and Israel. Each of these countries has consistently sought both to increase its inventories of advanced conventional weapons, and to build up the industrial infrastructure and technology base necessary to produce complex weapons. (The subject of the proliferation of military industry and technology is addressed in chapter 4.)

With respect to combat aircraft in particular, developing nations with large air forces also tend to have programs to develop nuclear, biological, and/or chemical weapons, and ballistic missiles. At the outset of the Persian Gulf War, for example, Iraq's air force comprised over 650 military aircraft, making it the fourth largest in the developing world, after China (with 5,780), North Korea (798), and India (796). This tendency is especially troubling as it is not unlikely that a military aircraft would be the delivery vehicle of choice for a nuclear or biological weapon originating in the developing world.[16]

From a technical standpoint, many military aircraft were specifically designed to accommodate and deliver nonconventional ordnance, and almost any combat aircraft with an attachment point on its wing can be modified for this purpose. Table 2.2 lists the twenty developing countries with the largest air forces. The column on the right indicates whether the country is suspected of having or developing weapons of mass destruction and/or ballistic missiles. Of the twenty countries, fifteen possess or are thought to have programs to develop weapons of mass destruction. If ballistic missiles are included, that number rises to eighteen.

Although it would be possible to deliver a nuclear weapon using a cart drawn by an ox, in most cases weapons of mass destruction must be mated with competent means of delivery appropriate to the particular mission. The likelihood of successful delivery can vary significantly, depending on the kind of weapon, the nature of the target, local air defenses, pilot skill, weather conditions, and the military objective of the mission, among other factors. Compared to nuclear weapons, however, for most military missions, it is generally more difficult to deliver chemical or biological agents, many of which must be sprayed (or dispersed in submunitions) at slow speeds upwind of the target.* For these reasons, combat aircraft are

---

*In most cases where WMDs are used by terrorists, however, chemical and biological weapons would be easier to deliver than nuclear ones.

TABLE 2.2. COMBAT AIRCRAFT AND WMD PROGRAMS IN
DEVELOPING NATIONS, 1992 (BY SIZE OF AIR FORCE)*

Country	FGA	Fighter	Bomber	Total	WMD/M
China	600	4,600	630	5,830	NBCM
North Korea	346	387	81(?)	814(?)	NBCM
India	400	327	9	736	NM
Israel	169	479	0	648	NBCM
Syria	170	463	0	633	BCM
Taiwan	512	0	0	512	BC
Egypt	149	323	0	472	CM
Turkey	415	20	0	435	none
South Korea	265	128	0	393	M
Lybia	128	238	5	371	BCM
Pakistan	150	214	0	364	NM
Iraq	130	180	6	316	[NBCM]
Saudi Arabia	152	132	0	284	M
Iran	130	132	0	262	NBCM
South Africa	245	14	5	259	[N]M
Algeria	57	185	0	242	NM
Afghanistan	110	123	0	233	M
Brazil	200	18	0	218	[N]M
Singapore	149	38	0	187	none
Vietnam	60	125	0	185	C

Legend
N =   often reported as having or trying to acquire nuclear weapons
B =   often reported as having an offensive biological warfare program
C =   often reported as having an offensive chemical warfare capability
M =   suspected of having or developing ballistic missiles with a range of at
       least 300 km, and not a full member of the MTCR as of March 1993
FGA = fighter/ground attack aircraft
[] =   weapons program is thought to have been suspended or terminated
*Of all developing nations thought to have been engaged in the development
of WMDs, only three—Myanmar (Burma), Ethiopia, and Argentina—are not
listed in table 2.2.

Source: Adapted from U.S. Congress, Office of Technology Assessment (OTA), *Technologies Underlying Weapons of Mass Destruction*, OTA-BP-ISC-115 (Washington, D.C.: U.S. Government Printing Office, December 1993), p. 237, table 5.8. Based on information drawn from International Institute for Strategic Studies, *The Military Balance 1992–1993* (London: IISS, 1992), and selected newspaper accounts.

generally considered to be more effective in the dispersal of chemical and biological weapons than are missiles.

As recent studies and the data in tables 2.2 and 2.3 suggest, many developing nations either possess or can buy advanced fighters and strike aircraft that are superior to available missiles—with respect to payload, accuracy, range, and reliability, among other characteristics.[17] A major congressional study concluded in 1993 that combat aircraft can be used to deliver weapons of mass destruction "effectively under most circumstances, usually even in the presence of significant air defenses."[18] In addition, there are many more combat aircraft than longer-range ballistic or cruise missiles in the developing world, and many more countries have them.

Most advanced industrial states subscribe to the principle of limiting the spread of missiles and the technologies, both military and commercial, that could contribute to the development of new missiles or the modification of existing ones. Most are parties to the MTCR. Trade in longer-range ballistic and cruise missiles is not considered a legitimate business, although there is an active trade in many other kinds of missiles, and in dual-use technologies that can be useful, or even prerequisite, in the development of WMD-capable cruise missiles. Most nations appear to be increasingly willing to impose diplomatic or economic sanctions to contain the spread of ballistic and cruise missiles above a specified range and payload.

By contrast, the proliferation of combat aircraft as potential delivery vehicles for weapons of mass destruction would appear to be an intractable problem. All countries with advanced arms industries actively support the efforts of their aerospace companies to make international sales. In 1995, for example, the Clinton administration announced its support of U.S. arms exports, specifically including combat aircraft:

TABLE 2.3. COMBAT AIRCRAFT ORDERED 1987–92 BY
COUNTRIES OF PROLIFERATION CONCERN

Country	WMD/M	No.	Type of Aircraft	Supplier	Year
China	NBCM	12	SU-24 Fencer	USSR	1990
		24	SU-24 Flanker	USSR	1991
		40	MiG-29	USSR	1991
North Korea	NBCM	20	SU-25 Frogfoot	USSR	1987
		25	MiG-29	USSR	1987
		150	MiG-21MF	USSR	1989
India	NM	15	MiG-29	USSR	1987
		15	Jaguar	UK/France	1988
		10	Sea Harrier	UK	1989
Israel	NBCM	30	F-16C	US	1988
		30	F-16C	US	1988
		15	F-15A Eagle	US	1990
		10	F-15A Eagle	US	1991
Taiwan	BC	34	Kfir-C7	Israel	1991
		6	Kfir-TC7	Israel	1991
		150	F-16	US	1992
		60	Mirage 2000-5	France	1992
Lybia	BCM	15	SU-24	USSR	1988
Syria	BCM	?	SU-24 Fencer	USSR	1988
		8	MiG-25	USSR	1989
South Korea	M	24	F-4D Phantom	US	1987
		4	F-16D	US	1988
		24	F-4E Phantom	US	1988
		12	RF-4C Phantom	US	1988
		24	F-4E Phantom	US	1989
		120	F/A-18 Hornet	US	1989
		9	RF-4C Phantom	US	1990
		120	F-16C	US	1991
Egypt	CM	42	F-16C	US	1987
		4	F-16D	US	1987
		1	F-16D	US	1988
		20	Mirage-2000	France	1988
		46	F-16C	US	1991

TABLE 2.3. *(continued)*

Country	WMD/M	No.	Type of Aircraft	Supplier	Year
Pakistan	NCM	11	F-16A	US	1988
		60	F-16A	US	1989
		75	F-7	China	1989
		50	Mirage-30	(Australia)	1990
Iraq	[NBCM]	36	Mirage F-1C	France	1987
		16	Mirage F-1C	France	1989
Brazil	[N]M	11	S2F-1	Canada	1987
		23	F-5E Tiger 2	US	1988
		6	Mirage 3-E	France	1988
Iran	NBCM	?	MiG-21F	(GDR)	1988
		?	MiG-29	USSR	1990
Saudi Arabia	M	12	F-15C Eagle	US	1987
		20	Hawk-200	UK	1988
		60	Hawk-100	UK	1990
		12	F-15D Eagle	US	1990
		72	F-15XP	US	1992
Algeria	NM	?	MiG-29	USSR	1988

Source: Adapted from OTA, *Technologies Underlying Weapons of Mass Destruction,* pp. 240–41, table 5.9; based on SIPRI Yearbooks, 1988–92 (New York: Oxford University Press, various years), and selected newspaper reports.

The United States will take such steps as tasking our overseas mission personnel to support overseas marketing efforts of American companies bidding on defense contracts, actively involving senior government officials in promoting sales of particular importance to the United States, and supporting official Department of Defense participation in international air and trade exhibitions.[19]

The market for fighters, both interceptors and strike aircraft, is extremely competitive. Proliferation of highly capable combat aircraft is increasing, and in the absence of a multilateral control regime, it is likely to get worse. Over the past several years, trade in military aircraft has been brisk. As Table 2.3 indicates, from 1987 through 1992 about 1,550 aircraft were ordered by nations thought to be engaged in the development of weapons of mass destruction and/or missiles.

All of the countries listed in table 2.3 that possess weapons of mass destruction already have the capability to deliver them to a variety of targets. In 1992, for example, the Pakistani air force consisted of approximately 364 fighter aircraft, including 21 Mirage-III and 58 Mirage-5 fighters. The Mirage-III is a second-generation, high-speed French fighter with a payload of 907 kg and combat radius of 1,200 km. The Mirage-5 is a somewhat more advanced aircraft with similar characteristics. About 150 of the Pakistani fighters are optimized for ground attack.

India, which boasts the third largest air force in the developing world, commands approximately 736 fighter aircraft, of which about 400 are configured for ground attack missions. The Indian air force includes 54 Soviet MiG-23s and 96 MiG-27s, which are third-generation, high-speed aircraft with payloads of 2,000 kg and a combat radius of roughly 700 km. Both India and Pakistan are widely thought to possess nuclear weapons, and the composition of their respective air forces indicates each could conduct a nuclear strike, which would likely involve a small number of warheads. Most of the countries of proliferation concern listed in tables 2.2 and 2.3 also have the capability to mount a significant strike, using chemical or biological agents, if they made appropriate modifications to combat aircraft already in their possession.

With respect to Pakistan, at least 28 of the F-16 fighter aircraft listed on table 2.3 were not delivered on schedule, even though Pakistan had paid over $600 million for them.[20] The aircraft were embargoed under the Pressler Amendment, which prohibits the sale or transfer of U.S. military equipment or technology to Pakistan unless the president of the United States certifies that Pakistan does not possess a nuclear device.[21] In 1990, when President George Bush did not make the required certification, all sales and military cooperation were put on hold. By 1995, however, in an effort to improve relations with Pakistan, the Clinton administration sought a one-time exception to the Amendment. They hoped to deliver a portion of the approximately $1.4 billion in arms that Pakistan had ordered in the late 1980s as part of their agenda to normalize relations with Islamabad.

Senator Larry Pressler (R-S.D.) responded that, according to a CIA briefing, Pakistan was in possession of nine or ten assembled nuclear weapons. In his view, making the exception would "offend the Indians, accelerate the arms race in South Asia and could lead to nuclear war."[22] Pressler's concerns were subsequently augmented by the disclosure that Pakistan is quietly building a 40-megawatt heavy water reactor that could produce significant amounts of plutonium, although Pakistan is probably still unable to reprocess the plutonium into weapons-grade fissile material. Moreover, because Pakistan is constructing the reactor with largely indigenous technology, it would not be subject to inspections by the International Atomic Energy Agency.[23] In a press conference with President Clinton on April 11, 1995, Pakistani Prime Minister Benazir Bhutto categorically denied that her country possessed a nuclear weapon.

The trade in combat aircraft is a particularly striking example of the tension among the military, economic, and political aspects of proliferation. It is now clear that in military terms, combat aircraft represent the most widespread and effective means of conveying a weapon of mass destruction (or any other weapon) to its target.[24] It is just as clear, however, that these weapons platforms continue to be proliferated because they are commodities in the international trade, and because foreign sales help to recoup investments that producers must make in developing them. Politically, combat aircraft are used, although with decreasing returns, in a foreign policy context—to reward friends and in largely ill-fated attempts to establish a military balance among potential combatants.

In time, it is likely that the political benefits of exporting combat aircraft will be exhausted or exposed as far less than meets the eye. With ready suppliers on all sides it is difficult to argue that approval or denial of a particular arms sale has the political cachet that once was claimed. If you cannot get a particular military capability from the United States, then you can probably get it from Russia. And in the unlikely event that both refuse, you can almost always get it from France, or from a number of other largely indiscriminate suppliers.

With decreased political value, the military and economic aspects of proliferation of combat aircraft take on greater weight. But as suggested above, it makes little sense for nations to export ground attack aircraft, especially to countries of proliferation concern, because it is not unlikely that such aircraft would figure prominently in a strike involving weapons of mass destruction. Moreover, as additional developing countries acquire capable air forces, it is increasingly likely that those weapons will be turned against the forces of one or more of the principal arms-exporting nations. It is little wonder that few military officers of flag rank view the arms trade with much enthusiasm. Even in the more mundane world of conventional warfare, suppression of enemy air power is always a critical objective.

In recent years, the major arms-producing states have had to face their own weapons, or those of their closest allies, in battle. This circumstance should create a military presumption against the export of large numbers of advanced fighter aircraft. After all, one arms-exporting nation cannot control the arms transfers of another, and, as the Persian Gulf War demonstrated, one state's customer is another's nemesis.

For these reasons, a large part of the final justification must be an economic one. This is hardly surprising given the astronomic cost of developing combat aircraft, which in the context of shrinking domestic markets has made it all but impossible for most nations to develop a post–cold war fighter. These circumstances have caused some politicians and military planners to question the need to undertake such programs. But the apparent imperative to export is, nevertheless, very significant in understanding the similar and perhaps more deep-seated problem of implementing effective export controls on commercial products that also have military applications.

THE DUAL-USE CONUNDRUM

If economic considerations drive the trade in combat aircraft in spite of the danger it presents, then it would seem that the economy must also prevail in any effort to stem the distribution of so-called dual-use technologies and commodities. The United States is of particular interest here for two reasons: first, as the leader of the free world, the United States took the initiative in establishing export controls; and second, Washington created a separate economy for developing military technology and procuring weapon systems.

After the Second World War, the United States government encouraged the development of two relatively separate industrial sectors, one commercial and the other military. Business practices in the two diverged significantly, and substantial barriers were established that tended to impede the transfer of technology between one sector and the other. These barriers, however, resulted from legal, institutional, and administrative arrangements, and were not inherent in the technologies themselves.[25]

Unlike other advanced industrial states, the United States made extraordinary efforts to differentiate technology as either military or commercial in character. This was possible largely because anti-Soviet ideology (combined with unprecedented national wealth) ensured political support to dedicate enormous financial, educational, industrial, and human resources to militarily specific R&D and the production of weapon systems. Other countries, such as Japan and Germany, pursued weapons development strategies that drew on American technology, broader international collaboration, and technology developed jointly for commercial and military purposes.

For much of the cold war, American defense analysts argued that technology naturally diffused from military development programs to the civil sector, a process they called "spin-off." The validity of spin-off rested on several assumptions: that military technology was more advanced than civil technology; that technology developed for military purposes could be modified for civil applications; and that the natural direction of technology transfer was from the military to commercial industry. In part, the concept of spin-off was an attempt to explain the relationship between the military and civilian applications of technology. But it was also frequently invoked to justify the escalating costs of weapon systems on the grounds that such expenditures contributed to the vitality of the U.S. economy.

But in the late 1980s, as the international economy became more highly integrated or global in many high-technology sectors, the spin-off argument lost force and credibility. In military circles, the term *spin-off* was replaced with *civil-military integration* and *spin-on*. The new terms embodied the recognition that many military applications of technology now lagged their civil counterparts. The traditional understanding of the direction of technology transfer was reversed. As the commercial sector forged ahead, military planners and analysts in Washington argued that it had become necessary to combine the technological attributes of both civil and military R&D to afford the next generation of weapon systems.[26]

These changes reflected a growing recognition that the United States no longer possessed sufficient resources or political will to push military technology uphill by brute force. In the future, the U.S. military would have to rely on the creative energies of vastly larger commercial sectors of the international economy.[27] As it turned out, declining U.S. competitiveness and technology leadership in some industries combined to increase reliance on foreign suppliers for parts and components for U.S. military equipment.

As warfare became more information-intensive throughout the 1980s, Japanese semiconductors and packaging materials produced for commercial markets increasingly found their way into U.S. missile guidance systems, so-called "smart" weapons, and a variety of weapons platforms. The use of commercial technologies and products is typical of the way in which Japan pursues military development programs. Indeed, the Japanese, and to a large extent, the Europeans, never accepted the spin-off model, and so did not organize their industries or regulatory structures to support it.

The dual-use character of the underlying technologies for nuclear, chemical, and biological weapons is perhaps the most striking of all. Commercial industries that are often associated with these weapons also represent a major segment in the political economy of the development of nations. Nuclear power, modern chemicals, and pharmaceuticals not only raise the standard of living for local populations, but also are important concomitants to attracting trade and investment within the global economy. For this reason, the process of development itself poses a challenge to nonproliferation.

Although proliferation of weapons of mass destruction is not technologically or economically determined, diffusion of the technologies associated with nuclear materials, chemical production processes, pharmacology, and aerospace to less developed nations compounds the problem of devising and implementing effective control regimes. Moreover, some states, notably Germany and France, have adopted export policies with respect to dual-use commodities that have made it far easier for developing states to make weapons of mass destruction. Both German and French firms, for example, directly contributed to the Iraqi program to develop biological and toxin weapons.[28]

Biotechnology and pharmacology are the base-disciplines both for the design of wonder drugs and vaccines, and for the production of biological and toxin weapons. Any state that could develop a pharmaceutical industry, or even operate foreign-supplied pharmaceutical plants and commercial fermentation facilities, could also develop biological agents. Officials of one major pharmaceutical company confirmed that the manufacture of significant quantities of deadly biological agents in facilities comparable to theirs would be technically "trivial."[29] According to one authoritative study:

Virtually all the equipment underlying production of biological and toxin agents has civil applications and has become widely available as fermentation technology, and the pharmaceutical and biotechnology industries more generally, have spread worldwide. Since militarily significant quantities of biological agents could be produced in a short time in small factories, they could be used offensively without the need for long-term stockpiles.[30]

Modern chemical plants can convert to produce chemical warfare agents, although the process can be time-consuming and cumbersome. And many chemical processes common to the industry are also used in manufacturing chemical weapons. In some cases, widely produced and distributed chemical precursors can be rapidly transformed into chemical weapons; in others, more processing is required. The base technologies underlying chemical weapons were proven in the First World War, although many refinements and new agents have been made over the years. There are literally thousands of chemical production sites worldwide, and the chemical industry is characterized by unusually high levels of cross-border direct investment, suggesting the global nature of its products and processes.

In the case of nuclear weapons, the greater part of the technical difficulty resides in producing sufficient amounts of highly enriched uranium or plutonium, unless these materials can be secured through the black market or diverted from the nuclear power industry into a weapons program. Many analysts believe that inadequate control of existing materials constitutes the greatest threat. The Soviet Union, for example, alone produced an estimated 500 to 1,000 tons of highly enriched uranium and 100 to 150 tons of plutonium. Russia and the three other nuclear inheritor states—Belarus, Kazakhstan, and Ukraine—lack adequate systems to account for and safeguard fissile materials.[31] As nuclear weapons now stored in these former Soviet Republics are dismantled or sent to Russia under terms of the Lisbon Protocol to the START I Treaty, more and more of this material will have to be stockpiled and stored in perpetuity.

Nuclear weapons can be extraordinarily complex, but they can also be rather rudimentary. The basic technologies were demonstrated against civilian populations over fifty years ago. Most states that have functioning nuclear power plants today understand how to generate and handle nuclear materials. They would also have the technological sophistication to design and build a simple gun-type nuclear weapon. In such a device, a propellant charge is used to drive two subcritical masses of highly enriched uranium together, forming a supercritical mass which can sustain a nuclear chain reaction, releasing tremendous amounts of energy. An implosion-type nuclear weapon is more difficult to develop, because very precisely timed detonations are necessary to compress subcritical masses of uranium or a plutonium pit to form the supercritical mass. Neither design, however, is beyond the range of most nations engaged in a significant nuclear power program.

Finally, modern information-intensive warfare depends on high-technology products from the electronics, semiconductor, computing, and telecommunications industries. These will increasingly be embedded in global (all-weather) surveillance systems, ballistic missile defense, precision guided weapons, real-time C3I systems, and systems that identify mobile targets as friend or foe (IFF), among others.* Here, even the Japanese, who have long prohibited the export of military equipment, can exert only marginal control over companies and political authorities that would use their high-technology products for military purposes.

The dual-use conundrum, that technology can be applied to both peaceful and military ends, will not go away. This is not a techno-

---

*C3I stands for "command, control, communications, and intelligence." IFF is for "identification friend or foe."

logically deterministic principle; rather, the use of technology for military applications has more to do with human understanding and will than it does with innate properties of technology. There are some few technologies that have purely military applications. Stealth technology, for example, is incompatible with commercial air traffic control, where the object is to increase aircraft signatures to avoid collision. But beyond such ludicrous examples, the use of technology for military purposes is always a political act. And it is the political sphere, not the technological one, where change and development are necessary.

REALIST FICTIONS

Suppose, then, that it is reasonable to assume that many states could acquire or learn to make and deliver weapons of mass destruction, that we are living in a post-proliferation age, and that if such weapons are not widespread today, they could be in ten or twenty years. As the cases of Algeria, China, Egypt, India, Iran, Iraq, Israel, Libya, North Korea, Pakistan, Syria, Taiwan, Vietnam, and others already attest, the alternative assumption, that some states should possess an oligopoly on the most powerful weapons, is increasingly difficult to sell to the developing world.*

Some analysts look not with dismay on this situation, but instead advocate a relaxation of traditional nonproliferation policies. For many years, writers of the realist school of international relations have argued that proliferation of nuclear weapons might actually increase the chances for stability, order, and peace.[32] They assert that

---

*For a listing of the WMD, missiles, and combat aircraft capabilities of these countries, see table 2.2.

international relations are inherently anarchical, that nations have historically sought to dominate their neighbors, and that states are readily deterred from aggression only when they believe they will be gravely punished for it.

According to the theory of deterrence, the threat of escalating war and massive destruction brought peace to Europe after the Second World War. The same logic is now being applied by some realist writers to the developing world. These are dangerous ideas, not only because they are hypothetical, but because they legitimize the efforts of all states to acquire weapons of mass destruction. Moreover, the realists' perspective has been used by a generation of policy makers to justify the position that monumental preparations for war must take precedence over efforts to establish stronger diplomatic and economic ties among states.[33]

One realist writer has argued in both the academic journals and the popular press that "the United States should encourage the limited and carefully managed proliferation of nuclear weapons in Europe."[34] He would stop at Germany, but if that proved impossible, as he thinks it might, "the current nuclear powers should let proliferation occur in Eastern Europe while doing all they can to channel it in safe directions."[35]

Realists have not always been so circumspect. In proposing the spread of nuclear weapons in the developing world, one prominent academic even found it necessary to minimize the significance of their use: "If such states use nuclear weapons, the world will not end. And the use of nuclear weapons by lesser powers would hardly trigger them elsewhere," a position that he continues to advocate.[36] Another nuclear apologist suggests that acquisition of such weapons by developing nations "can represent no more than strategic 'pinpricks' to the superpowers," and in any case, that "nuclearization of regional conflict patterns in the third world will tend to be self-regulating."[37]

A single-minded focus on the distribution of military power under the cold war assumption of U.S.-Soviet competition led the realists to a limited concept of proliferation. Nuclear weapons became the centerpiece in a dark theology in which the credible threat of absolute annihilation was the only means to impose order on an inherently chaotic political universe. The world is certainly more complicated now.

In the hands of a superpower, for example, biological and toxin weapons are the functional equivalent of nuclear ones, if the goal is to destroy mass populations. Both the United States and the Soviet Union mastered the production, weaponization, and delivery of biological agents a generation ago. But the realists overlooked the power of biological weapons. This was an important omission because the technologies underlying biological weapons are widespread, easy to develop, and relatively inexpensive. In stemming the proliferation of biological weapons, one cannot count on technological hurtles to slow the process, or on finding a trail that might be left though procurement of forbidden components or processes.

Nevertheless, if realist logic applies to nuclear weapons, it would also have to apply to these weapons. Would it then make sense to encourage the "carefully managed" spread of biological weapons? The advocates of nuclear proliferation find themselves in the awkward position of having to answer this question in the affirmative. But breaking down the norm or inhibition against the production and weaponization of biological and toxin agents could result in many additional nations acquiring these capabilities, and because biological weapons would probably be developed in secret, they would have little deterrent effect.

In the aftermath of the cold war, the advanced industrial world is increasingly ordered by treaty, by contract, by economic liberalization, and by cross-border investments of multinational corporations. Foreign direct investment has grown by a factor of four over the past decade to reach $2 trillion.[38] While direct investment, trade, and more integrated capital markets do not guarantee peace and security, the ordered international economic and political relations they entail offer more hope of averting war than the weapons that some possess and others do not.[39]

For the foreseeable future, the burden of public policy must focus on the political instability and military ambitions of many states in the developing world, as well as the impact that proliferation, broadly defined, will have on the frequency and severity of regional conflicts. The arms buildup among China, Taiwan, India, and Pakistan—for example—continues to escalate,[40] amid concerns voiced by the U.S. intelligence community that Iraq, China, Syria, Iran, Egypt, Taiwan, and Libya have secretly continued or reinstated biological weapons programs, in clear violation of the Biological and Toxin Weapons Convention.[41]

Ever increasing levels of military capability in the developing world also raise the stakes associated with U.S. policy on the transfer of conventional arms. As the only remaining superpower, the progenitor and harbinger of military technology, and the world's leading arms merchant, the United States has a special part to play in the drama. In chapter 3, the global arms trade is examined with particular attention to American practices and leadership on arms exports to the Middle East after the Persian Gulf War. The implications of that trade and of American policy do not bode well for peace and stability in the less developed world.

3 AN AVALANCHE OF ARMS

AFTER THE COLD WAR

In the summer and fall of 1991 the Iraqi invasion of Kuwait tarnished the image of the "new world order." It also failed to add coherence or intelligence to the arms export and military industrial policies of the United States and Europe. Perhaps because the U.S.-led coalition emerged victorious, with few casualties and with such apparent ease, the contradictions and realities enveloping the 1991 Gulf War failed to register on policy makers in the West. International production of weapons and transfer of military technology continued to expand, and U.S. arms exports flourished. The opportunity to comprehend and implement a critical redirection of international relations was delayed and probably lost.

At the end of the cold war, it might have been possible to create an effective multilateral regime to constrain the flow of arms and military technology to developing nations. It would have required sustained leadership by the United States and a minimum of compliance and cooperation from the European powers and Russia because these nations are responsible for 90 percent of the trade in arms, a trade in which the vast majority (78 percent) of weapons is imported by developing nations. (See table 3.6.)

The Persian Gulf War graphically demonstrated the consequences of extensive commerce in modern conventional weapons; and because it exposed many contradictions and complexities obscured by the cold war, it also provided an opportunity for diplomacy. At the same time it demonstrated the superiority of American weapons, increasing demand for them, principally in the Middle East and East Asia.

During the 1991 Gulf War and in its aftermath, the region and the world were bombarded with tales and images of Patriots knocking Scuds from the sky, of U.S. cluster bombs taking out Iraqi missile defenses, and of precision guided munitions flying through open windows or killing tanks on bridges.[1] In the Gulf, the American military cast off the pall of Vietnam, and the prospects for export of American weapons brightened. A discussion of the data on international arms transfers, and on the processes by which the United States exports weapons, is necessary to assess the dramatic increase of U.S. arms exports to the Middle East following the Persian Gulf War.

The United States exports weapons on two basic tracks: one public, the other private. In the first, the Foreign Military Sales (FMS) program, the U.S. government sponsors the sale. It is administered by the Defense Security Assistance Agency (DSAA). Typically the

DSAA helps line up the customer, negotiates the agreement with the foreign government, collects the money, arranges with U.S. companies to produce the weapons, transfers the weapons, and may even provide for after-sales service and spare parts.[2] The foreign government must pay for the weapons in advance of their production. In essence, the FMS program avails the military procurement apparatus of the United States to foreign governments. To that end, the DSAA maintains parallel procurement operations within the so-called "buying commands" of the U.S. Army, Navy, and Air Force.

The nature and scope of FMS agreements vary, but a single agreement can result, for example, in the production and export of hundreds of advanced tanks, fighter aircraft, or precision guided munitions. The DSAA may also arrange for coproduction of weapons, where the underlying manufacturing technologies are transferred to foreign governments and companies for local production. Many foreign governments historically have preferred the FMS route because it ensures the full backing of the U.S. government, although it does add 3 percent to the cost of the weapons for DSAA administration of the contract.

This 3 percent fee became the focus of controversy in the early 1990s because the high volume of arms sales left the agency awash in foreign money, funds that had not been appropriated and could not therefore be controlled by Congress. In addition, the agency's funding is directly tied to its success in securing sales of U.S. military equipment to foreign governments. Accordingly, DSAA personnel stationed at U.S. embassies and field offices around the world have a strong incentive to ferret out and negotiate arms deals with foreign governments.[3] In 1994, 2,085 U.S. government civilian employees and 5,766 U.S. contract employees were involved in implementing U.S. military sales in 105 foreign countries.[4] These considerations prompted Congress to place a $300-million cap on the funds that the agency could accumulate in its FMS 3 percent fee account.[5]

The FMS program represents a substantial part—but far from the total—of U.S. arms exports because it does not include the second track, that is, direct commercial sales (DCS) by U.S. arms companies to foreign governments and corporations. In a commercial sale, U.S. arms companies find the foreign customer, negotiate the contract, and apply to the State Department for a license to export military items that are controlled by the U.S. Munitions List. If the license is granted, it is valid for four years, and the sale is then conducted as a private business transaction largely outside the purview of the U.S. government.

Although direct commercial export of U.S. weapons began in the thirties, it did not become a major factor until 1981, when Congress abolished limitations on the dollar amount of weapons that could be exported using commercial channels. According to one Washington source, "Between 1950 and 1980, only $10.4 billion of weapons were exported under DCS licenses, but during the next ten years, nearly four times that amount ($38.5 billion) were delivered."[6]

DSAA data distinguish among (a) FMS *agreements*, in which a foreign government places an order with the DSAA for military equipment or technology; (b) FMS *deliveries*, in which equipment or technology is delivered to a foreign government pursuant to an FMS agreement; and (c) direct commercial sales (DCS), in which equipment and technology are delivered to a foreign government or corporation directly from a U.S. arms maker. The State Department maintains a register of controlled military items, the U.S. Munitions List. U.S. companies must apply for a license prior to exporting any military item on the list.

Table 3.1, which is based almost entirely on DSAA data, shows the relative importance of government-sponsored arms exports (FMS deliveries, column 3) and arms exported directly by industry (DCS deliveries, column 6). FMS deliveries increased by about $1 billion a year after 1990, and DCS deliveries appear to have decreased by about the same amount. On its face, table 3.1 would seem to indicate that the volume of U.S. arms exports has not been affected much either by the performance of U.S. weapons in the Persian Gulf or by the end of the cold war. Although the two categories vary from one year to the next (columns 3 and 6), when they are added together, there appears to be overall continuity of U.S. arms exports between 1984 and 1993 (see column 7).

But the numbers are misleading. U.S. arms exports in fact increased dramatically in the early 1990s. In 1995, we were still waiting for the statistics to catch up with the facts. The rise in U.S. arms exports following the Persian Gulf War is presaged by a corresponding increase in the level of *agreements* to sell weapons over the same period (column 2).

As table 3.2 indicates, the end of the cold war brought with it a rough doubling of U.S. *agreements* to export arms under the FMS program. In fiscal years 1991 through 1994, U.S. government-sponsored FMS agreements mushroomed to a total of $83.1 billion, up from $34.5 billion, the total for fiscal years 1986 through 1989. In fiscal year 1993, U.S. FMS agreements reached a record high of $33.2 billion. That number included 72 F-15 fighter aircraft for Saudi Arabia, 150 F-16 fighters for Taiwan, and 256 MIA2 tanks for Kuwait, among hundreds of other deals.

These arrangements are not reflected as FMS *deliveries* (column 3) in table 3.1 because it takes several years for the DSAA to order, procure, and deliver major weapon systems to its foreign customers. It

TABLE 3.1. FMS AND DCS AGREEMENTS, DELIVERIES, AND
LICENSES, 1984–94 ($ BILLIONS, CURRENT YEAR)

Year	FMS Agreements	FMS Deliveries		DCS Licenses	DCS Deliveries	FMS + DCS Deliveries	
(1)	(2)	(3)	(4)	(5)	(6)	(7)	(8)
1984	12.8	9.7	8.2	nd	3.4	13.1	11.6
1985	11.3	8.4	7.5	nd	5.1	13.5	12.6
1986	6.3	7.8	7.2	nd	3.7	11.5	10.9
1987	6.3	11.1	10.8	nd	6.5	17.6	17.3
1988	11.6	9.2	8.8	nd	4.8	14.0	13.6
1989	10.3	7.4	7.1	nd	8.5	15.9	15.6
1990	12.3	7.8	7.5	nd	6.2	14.0	13.7
1991	21.6	9.0	8.6	39.1	5.0	14.0	13.6
1992	15.4	10.6	10.3	16.0	2.5	13.1	12.8
1993	33.2	11.6	11.2	26.5	3.2	14.8	14.4
1994	12.9*	nd	nd	25.6†	nd	nd	nd

Legend
(4) = FMS deliveries less military construction
(8) = FMS plus DCS deliveries less military construction
nd = no data
* DSAA Memorandum for Correspondents, no. 288-M, Nov. 10, 1994.
† Office of Defense Trade Controls, State Department, "Licenses/Approvals for the Export of Commercially Sold Defense Articles/Services as of 30 September 1994."

Source: Data on FMS agreements, FMS deliveries, and DCS deliveries are from U.S. Department of Defense, Defense Security Assistance Agency (DSAA), *Foreign Military Sales, Foreign Military Construction Sales and Military Assistance Facts* (Washington, D.C.: FMS Control & Reports Division, Comptroller, DSAA, September 30, 1993), pp. 1–3, 15–17, 24–25, 52–53. Data on DCS licenses are from *Congressional Record*, January 24, 1992, p. E67; and *Congressional Record*, April 21, 1993, p. E971.

TABLE 3.2. U.S. FOREIGN MILITARY SALES AGREEMENTS, FISCAL
YEARS 1986–94 ($ BILLIONS, CURRENT YEARS)

Cold War Years					After the Cold War			
1986	1987	1988	1989	(1990)	1991	1992	1993	1994
6.3	6.3	11.6	10.3	(12.3)	21.6	15.4	33.2	12.9
	34.5			transition to post–cold war			83.1	

Source: DSAA, *Foreign Military Sales, Foreign Military Construction Sales, and Military Assistance Facts*, pp. 1–3. Data for 1994 is from DSAA Memorandum for Correspondents, no. 288-M, Nov. 10, 1994.

is, therefore, quite likely that U.S. government–sponsored arms exports (FMS *deliveries*) will rise dramatically between 1995 and 2000, based on the spectacular rise in the level of FMS *agreements* in the early and mid-1990s.

In most years, the dollar value of FMS *agreements* exceeds the dollar value of equipment actually delivered under the FMS program (compare columns 2 and 3, table 3.1). This is because about one-sixth of the contracts are not consummated, and actual deliveries of a single contract may be spread out over several fiscal years. There is, nevertheless, a direct and measurable relationship between FMS agreements to buy weapons and FMS deliveries of weapons to foreign governments: on average, approximately 84 percent of the weapons ordered are in fact delivered to the customer.[7] It is, accordingly, not unreasonable to expect that the $83.1 billion in agreements negotiated by the Bush administration in the three years following the Persian Gulf War will result in the export of roughly $70 billion in weapons and military technology, principally to developing nations in the Middle East and East Asia.

What about the other channel (DCS *deliveries*), those weapons that are exported directly by U.S. firms to foreign governments? Reported commercial military sales rose steadily in the 1980s to reach a high of $8.5 billion in 1989, but tapered off to an average of about $4.2 billion a year for the first four years of the 1990s. Data on direct commercial sales are compiled by the Office of Defense Trade Controls, using shippers' export documents and completed license forms returned to the State Department by the U.S. Customs Service. The process is extremely cumbersome, and it often takes two to three years for a sale to be reflected in the yearly total.

For this reason, the figures in table 3.1 on DCS *deliveries* (column 6) are likely to be revised substantially upward over the next two years. The Office of Defense Trade Controls "estimates future exports to be between 40 and 60 percent of the actual dollar value of licenses approved in the two previous fiscal years."[8] If this estimate is correct, then the large volume of licenses issued—$39.1 billion in 1991, $16.0 billion in 1992, $26.5 billion in 1993, and $25.6 billion in 1994—will result in a steep increase in the volume of direct commercial sales (table 3.1, column 6) in subsequent years.

These two factors combined—expected increases in FMS deliveries based on high levels of FMS agreements, and likely growth in DCS deliveries based on the volume of DCS licenses—should produce record levels of total U.S. arms exports in the last half of the 1990s. Based on DSAA data, the United States is likely to be first or second among the world's largest and most successful arms merchants well into the late 1990s and beyond. Indeed, the U.S. Department of Defense forecast the annual average level of U.S. arms exports to be $16 billion from 1994 through the year 2000.[9] If this forecast proves reliable, the yearly total for U.S. arms exports would exceed all previous years except two. As figure 3.1 indicates, in 1973 and 1987, U.S. arms exports totaled $19.7 and $17.4 billion, respectively.

Data published by the Defense Security Assistance Agency on U.S. arms exports are probably the most accurate because that agency administers the U.S. arms export program. But DSAA data are limited because they do not include export information for other countries. By contrast, data published by the U.S. Arms Control and Disarmament Agency (ACDA) cover the arms exports and imports of 144 nations, but much of it is based on estimates and guesswork, and it is sometimes out of date.

In addition, the quality of the ACDA data varies considerably, depending on the countries described; data on U.S. arms transfers are the most accurate, because they are drawn from official U.S. government sources. Data for European and NATO countries are somewhat less accurate but still reliable, because they are estimates based on official information provided by close U.S. allies. Even so, it takes several years for the European data to be collected and made available to the ACDA. That is why ACDA figures are typically revised upward from year to year. For example, the 1991 figure for European NATO arms exports was estimated as $6.4 billion in March 1994, but grew to $9.9 billion by February 1995, an upward revision of about 55 percent.[10]

Data on the Soviet Union were harder to obtain than European data because the Soviets did not cooperate in the collection procedures. It is, accordingly, difficult to place much confidence in ACDA data regarding arms transfers by the Soviet Union and other former communist states. Moreover, no exchange rate mechanism operated between the communist and Western economic systems, Soviet arms transfers were shrouded in official government secrecy, and by ACDA's own account, the data presented "are approximations based on limited information."[11] In addition, it is not unlikely that data on the former Soviet Union were inflated during the cold war by the

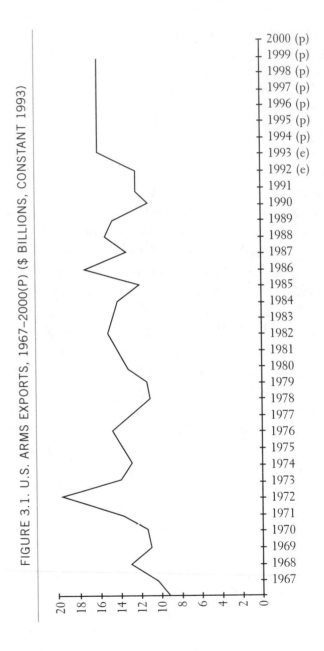

FIGURE 3.1. U.S. ARMS EXPORTS, 1967–2000(P) ($ BILLIONS, CONSTANT 1993)

Source: Data provided to the author by the Arms Control and Disarmament Agency (ACDA); (e) indicates that $2.0 billion has been added to the ACDA total as an estimate to correct for direct commercial sales not yet recorded; (p) indicates a number projected by the Department of Defense in the report entitled *World-Wide Conventional Arms Trade (1994–2000): A Forecast and Analysis* (Washington, D.C.: U.S. Department of Defense, December 1994), p. 55.

U.S. military and intelligence community sources that provided it. This does not suggest a deliberate disinformation campaign, only that great latitude existed both in methodology and in data collection techniques. Cold war assumptions and political judgments about the magnitude of the Soviet military threat would naturally have influenced guesswork about the extent and value of Soviet arms exports.

The limited accuracy of data on Soviet arms transfers has important implications for understanding the arms trade in recent years. As will be demonstrated below, the greatest decrease in the volume of world arms exports after the cold war is associated with a dramatic reduction in the arms transfers of Russia and the other former Soviet Republics. As it turns out, military exports in the West have declined only moderately, and U.S. arms exports may be increasing, if the Pentagon forecast cited above is correct.

With these caveats and limitations in mind, ACDA data can nevertheless be used to describe the context in which U.S. arms exporters came to dominate the global arms trade in the years leading up to and following the end of the cold war. With the collapse of Soviet communism (and Soviet arms sales), and increased preference for American weapons resulting from the Persian Gulf War, U.S. arms exporters found themselves in a commanding position.

In the ten years preceding the Persian Gulf War, 1981 through 1990, the United States exported a total of $144.0 billion in arms as compared to $149.8 billion for the European NATO powers combined. Overall the figures for the United States and Europe are remarkably similar, an average of $14.4 and $15.0 billion each year, respectively. As table 3.3 shows, the value of arms exported by the West began to decline in the late 1980s: combined exports fell from a total of $156.1 billion in the first half of the decade (1981–85), to a total of $137.7 billion in the second half (1986–90), a drop of $18.4 billion or about 11.8 percent.

But the decline was uneven, falling entirely on the European exporters, who sold $65.0 billion (1986–90) as compared to $84.8 billion in the previous five-year period, a drop of $19.8 billion or about 23 percent. In contrast, U.S. exports increased $.4 billion for the same period to reach $72.7 billion for 1986–90. U.S. arms exports stabilized at somewhat lower levels in the three years immediately following the end of the cold war, 1991–93. But according to ACDA officials, data for 1993 (and to a lesser extent, 1992 and 1991) are considerably understated because they tend not to include U.S. commercial arms transfers.[12] It may be that U.S. arms exports turned a corner in 1992 and are headed back up.

The decline of arms exports by the Soviet Union and other members of the Warsaw Treaty Organization (WTO) was more dramatic. As table 3.4 shows, Soviet weapons sales plummeted from $28.7 billion in 1987 to $7.0 billion in 1991. That year, the United States became the world's leading arms merchant, a position it would continue to enjoy and consolidate for the foreseeable future. As discussed above, a good deal of skepticism about the magnitude of Soviet arms sales is appropriate, both during and at the end of the cold war.

Table 3.4 also demonstrates the extent to which historically the world arms market was a cold war phenomenon. For the ten years prior to the Persian Gulf War, the combined exports of the NATO and WTO military alliances averaged 89 percent of all arms transfers worldwide. In 1990, that number reached 93 percent. At the same time, world arms exports fell from an average of $66.9 billion a year for the preceding ten years to $31.8 billion in 1991, or by

TABLE 3.3. ARMS EXPORTS OF THE U.S. AND NATO EUROPE, 1981–93 ($ BILLIONS, CONSTANT 1993)

Year	US	NATO Europe	Total
1981	13.5	17.2	30.7
1981	13.7	15.9	29.6
1983	15.2	15.0	30.2
1984	14.7	19.8	34.5
1985	14.2	16.9	31.1
1986	12.0	14.2	26.2
1987	17.4	14.5	31.9
1988	13.3	12.4	25.7
1989	15.4	10.7	26.1
1990	14.6	13.2	27.8
1991	11.4	9.9	21.3
1992	10.4	8.2	18.6
1993	10.3	7.0	17.3
Subtotal 1981–85	71.3	84.8	156.1
Subtotal 1986–90	72.7	65.0	137.7
Subtotal 1981–90	144.0	149.8	293.8
Total 1981–93	176.1	174.9	351
Average 1981–85	14.3	17.0	31.2
Average 1986–90	14.5	13.0	27.5
Average 1981–90	14.4	15.0	29.4

Source: Data for the years 1983–93 are from ACDA, *World Military Expenditures and Arms Transfers, 1993–1994* (Washington, D.C.: U.S. Government Printing Office, February 1995), pp. 98, 135. Data for the years 1981 and 1982 are from ACDA, *World Military Expenditures and Arms Transfers, 1991–1992* (Washington, D.C.: U.S. Government Printing Office, March 1994), pp. 90, 127; these data have been converted from current 1981 and 1982 dollars to constant 1993 dollars using a deflator provided by ACDA: 1993 = 1, 1981 = .6387, and 1982 = .6783.

TABLE 3.4. ARMS EXPORTS FOR NATO, WTO, AND THE WORLD,
1981–93 ($ BILLIONS, CONSTANT 1993)

Year	NATO	US	WTO	USSR	NATO + WTO	World	NATO + WTO /World
1981	31.0	13.5	32.1	27.9	63.1	69.8	90%
1981	30.2	13.7	32.7	27.9	62.9	72.7	87%
1983	30.8	15.2	32.1	27.6	62.9	69.8	90%
1984	35.3	14.7	31.1	26.4	66.4	76.6	87%
1985	31.8	14.2	28.6	22.8	60.4	65.9	92%
1986	26.9	12.0	32.8	27.5	59.7	65.3	91%
1987	32.7	17.4	33.7	28.7	66.4	74.4	89%
1988	26.4	13.3	31.0	27.0	57.4	67.3	85%
1989	26.6	15.4	24.7	22.6	51.3	58.1	88%
1990	28.4	14.6	17.4	16.8	45.8	49.5	93%
1991	21.7	11.4	7.4	7.0	29.1	31.8	92%
1992	19.6	10.4	2.6		22.2	24.7	90%
1993	17.5	10.3	2.8		20.3	22.0	92%
Average 1981–85	31.8	14.3	31.3	26.5	63.1	71.0	89%
Average 1986–90	28.2	14.5	27.9	24.5	56.1	62.9	89%
Average 1981–90	30.0	14.4	29.6	25.5	59.6	66.9	89%
Subtotal 1981–85	159.1	71.3	156.6	132.6	315.7	354.8	
Subtotal 1986–90	141.0	72.7	139.6	122.6	280.6	314.6	
Subtotal 1981–90	300.1	144.0	296.2	255.2	596.3	669.4	
Total 1981–93	358.9	176.1	309.0	262.2	667.9	747.9	

Source: Data for the years 1983–93 are from ACDA, *World Military Expenditures and Arms Transfers, 1993–1994*, pp. 91, 97, 98, 128, 130, 135. Data for the years 1981 and 1982 are from ACDA, *World Military Expenditures and Arms Transfers, 1991–1992*, pp. 89, 81, 93, 123, 127; these data have been converted from current 1981 and 1982 dollars to constant 1993 dollars using a deflator provided by ACDA: 1993 = 1, 1981 = .6387, and 1982 – .6783.

about 48 percent. For all exporting nations, except the United States, the bottom had literally dropped out of the international arms markets.

AMERICAN LEADERSHIP

Following the dramatic destruction of Iraqi military power, U.S. leaders found themselves in a position to exert profound influence on the course of conventional weapons proliferation. In one scenario, the United States could choose to press its advantage, to increase arms exports to a range of existing markets, particularly in the Middle East and East Asia. In another, as the leading arms exporter, the United States might have seized the moment to convince the other major suppliers to reduce commerce in weapons and advanced military technology.[13]

That choice pitted Congressional activism in the area of nonproliferation and conventional arms control against the ambitious arms export policies and plans of the Bush administration. In mid-September 1990, with U.S. forces deploying in the Persian Gulf but not yet engaged, the administration floated a proposal to sell approximately $21 billion in military equipment to Saudi Arabia. Even though the administration envisioned a sale of advanced equipment in unprecedented quantities, it failed to consult with key Congressional leaders. The reaction was predictable, strong and sustained. Subcommittee Chairman David R. Obey characterized the sale as "wildly large . . . grossly oversized."[14]

Within a week, the administration made a tactical decision to reduce the $21-billion proposal to $7.5 billion. In October, eleven senators denounced the sale on the Senate floor. Senator Alan Cranston accused the administration of misrepresenting its magnitude to

Congress. "At a Foreign Relations Committee hearing last week," he said, "the truth came out. The alleged smaller package turned out to be a fake. The proposed $7.5 billion sale is not to be a substitute for the big package. It is only a teaser, a forerunner of what would be the largest arms transfer in U.S. history."[15] On the House side, Foreign Affairs Subcommittee Chairman Lee H. Hamilton held a hearing in which he accused the administration of failing to "play this sale straight" with the Congress. "Let's be frank," he added, "while this package is a very big improvement over the first proposal, much of it still has nothing to do with the current crisis in Kuwait. . . . [T]he Saudis, with only 65,000 men under arms, will simply not be capable of defending themselves against a well-armed Iraq absent significant American support, no matter how gold-plated their equipment."[16]

In the months following the end of the 1991 Gulf War, Congressional proposals to curtail U.S. arms sales to the Middle East proliferated. In April, five influential members of the House of Representatives—Dante Fascell, Richard Gephardt, Lee Hamilton, David Obey, and Sam Gejdenson—wrote President Bush stating that "a temporary pause is necessary in order to facilitate multilateral negotiations on agreements to restrain the flow of sophisticated conventional weapons systems and other weapons technologies into this region."[17] Senator Joseph R. Biden, among others, held hearings on the possibility of creating an arms suppliers' cartel to restrict the transfer of weapons to the Middle East. Biden stated his view that the administration and the Congress "should be working together to ensure that the world does not return to business as usual in the Middle East. The central part," he said, "must be a concentrated effort to avoid new Middle East arms sales."[18]

It was in this context that President Bush announced in May 1991 a plan for arms control in the Middle East. It was the first major policy statement on proliferation issued by Washington following the Persian Gulf War. The president proposed a ban on weapons of mass destruction and a freeze on the acquisition, production, and testing of surface-to-surface missiles in the region. There was, of course, no possibility that Israel would agree to ban nuclear weapons, but restrictions on biological and chemical weapons and missiles might have been negotiable.

With respect to conventional arms, the plan called upon the five major suppliers—the United States, the Soviet Union, China, France, and Britain—to exercise "collective self restraint," to avoid exporting "destabilizing" weapons, and to draw up a set of guidelines for the transfer of conventional weapons to the Middle East.[19] At the time, these five powers together accounted for more than 90 percent of all arms exports to the developing world, and for an even higher percentage of trade in advanced weapons; they were also the five permanent members of the UN Security Council, although the plan was not associated with the United Nations.

In the press briefings and explanations that followed the announcement, the Bush administration made clear its intention to sell conventional weapons to the Middle East. "We are going to continue to provide for the legitimate defense interests of our friends and allies in the Middle East," one spokesman said, "to the extent that involves arms sales, we will proceed with them."[20] About a week later, Reginald Bartholomew, the undersecretary of state with responsibility for arms exports, explained the new policy to the Senate Foreign Relations Committee:

We do not believe that arms sales are necessarily destabilizing. Quite the contrary. . . . We will not seek a regime that halts arms transfers, but we have proposed one that will seek to ensure that sales that do take place are responsible. That is why, Mr. Chairman, it is in no way a contradiction for the United States to be simultaneously seeking an arms transfer regime with the other major suppliers and continuing to supply arms needed by peaceful States to defend themselves against aggressors.[21]

Several days prior to the hearing, the administration announced the sale of twenty Apache attack helicopters to the United Arab Emirates (UAE) and eight to Bahrain. When questioned, Bartholomew responded that the sale was not destabilizing. Quite the contrary, it was "consistent with what we are trying to do—politically, in security terms, and with this arms control proposal in the area." The sale was legitimate because, in his view, it did not introduce new levels of military capability, contribute to the regional arms race, or enable the UAE to project power into neighboring states. One senator asked if this meant that Apache-type attack gunships would therefore be allowable under the proposed arms control regime. His response: it depends entirely on the circumstance of the sale in question. Would advanced fighter aircraft be permissible? His answer: "I am not ready to say that there are no circumstances in which the transfer of advanced fighter aircraft could be stabilizing as opposed to destabilizing. It most certainly can be [stabilizing]." What could be banned by definition? Only weapons of mass destruction and ballistic missiles.[22]

What the undersecretary knew, but would not state for the record, was that the plan to control arms exports to the Middle East would not diminish the heavy flow of U.S. arms to that region. Quite the contrary, the Apache sale (valued at about $682 million) was only the first on a long list of planned exports to the Persian Gulf.[23] In this hearing, and others that followed, the administration merely went through the motions to ensure a compliant Congress. It had already set the policy agenda. The plan was to cement cooperative security arrangements among the smaller states of the Persian Gulf and provide the muscle to back them up. To do this, the United States would arm the Gulf—principally Saudi Arabia, Kuwait, Bahrain, Oman, and the United Arab Emirates (with the usual compliment of weapons for Israel and Egypt)—to unprecedented levels, and then be prepared to commit troops again if and when the weapons failed to deter or repel aggression from other highly armed states in the region. The role of the United States as security guarantor was critical because the administration never believed that its Persian Gulf clients, even when fully armed, could do more than slow the onslaught of a determined aggressor.

The illogic which informed the administration's policy operated at two levels—at the level of the individual sale and at the level of achieving a regional military balance through arms sales. This approach inverts the notion of a military balance associated with regional arms control treaties, where a balance is reached so that levels of arms can progressively be reduced in the context of confidence-building, monitoring, and verification. In the administration's view, individual sales could be stabilizing or destabilizing, responsible or irresponsible, depending on the circumstances. If the right combination of stabilizing sales could be made, theory had it, they would collectively contribute to a balance of military power, to regional stability, and ultimately to the protection of American interests in the Middle East. Bush and his closest advisers so fixed on the notion of achieving a balance that they terminated the attack at the height of the Persian Gulf War so as to preserve elements of Iraqi power in the region.

But this policy, which requires massive arms transfers to maintain or build up military power on all sides to achieve peace, even in the midst of war, is flawed. First, while any particular sale might be labeled stabilizing or destabilizing, stability is neither a fixed property nor an objective quality when applied to arms sales. It is not fixed because the designation "stabilizing" depends on circumstances which often change in unpredictable ways. Weapons sold for defensive purposes can be deployed in offensive configurations; they may be captured by opposing forces. It is not objective because what appears to be a stabilizing sale on one side may be interpreted as an aggressive new capability by the other, stimulating an arms race and further complicating the equation.

Second, the linkage between any particular arms sale and an overall balance of power in the Middle East is tenuous and time-limited at best. There is no single balance to be achieved in the region, but rather, a series of potential conflicts, which may or may not develop. There is the balance between Israel and certain of the Arab states, which, far from being maintained at equal levels, has been constructed to give Israel a qualitative superiority; in any case, Israel's possession of a large number of nuclear weapons and accurate means of delivery puts it in a class by itself. There is a balance between Egypt and several Arab states. There is also the balance in the Persian Gulf, which was the principal interest of the Bush administration, between the small oil-rich states and their larger, poorer, more belligerent neighbors to the north. Each of these relationships interacts with the others, making an overall balance very difficult to achieve.

One commentator has characterized the region as one in which the leaders of most key countries "believe they are surrounded by enemies, facing a military threat from virtually every direction, and thus, must arm accordingly."[24] Under such conditions, the Persian Gulf War can be seen—at a very fundamental level—as a correction of the military imbalance in the Persian Gulf created by profligate and irresponsible arms sales to Iraq and Iran in the 1980s. Table 3.5 shows the magnitude of arms imports by those states.

Third, the American policy to use massive arms transfers to reach a balance in the Persian Gulf was unilateral in nature, and it did not and could not anticipate or compensate for arms transferred by other nations. Wide and increasing diversity of supply, from both advanced and developing nations, has degraded the use of arms

TABLE 3.5. ARMS IMPORTED BY IRAQ AND IRAN, 1979–93
($ BILLIONS, CONSTANT 1993)

Year	Iraq	Iran	Total
1979	5.8	2.8	8.6
1980	4.1	0.7	4.8
1981	6.7	1.4	8.1
1982	10.5	2.4	12.9
1983	9.8	1.2	11.0
1984	12.7	3.7	16.4
1985	6.4	2.5	8.9
1986	7.7	3.3	11.0
1987	7.3	2.5	9.8
1988	6.6	3.1	9.7
1989	2.6	1.6	4.2
1990	3.1	2.0	5.1
1991	0.0	2.2	2.2
1992	0.0	0.4	0.4
1993	0.0	1.0	1.0
Total	83.3	30.8	114.1

Source: Data for the years 1983–93 are from ACDA, *World Military Expenditures and Arms Transfers, 1993–1994*, p. 115. Data for the years 1981 and 1982 are from ACDA, *World Military Expenditures and Arms Transfers, 1991–1992*, p. 109. The data for the years 1979–82 have been converted from current 1979–82 dollars to constant 1993 dollars using a deflator provided by ACDA: 1993 = 1, 1979 = .5309, 1980 = .5808, 1981 = .6387, and 1982 = .6783.

transfers—and their denial—as instruments of foreign policy. When the U.S. Congress blocked the sale of F-15 fighters to Saudi Arabia in the mid-1980s, for example, the Saudis were able to buy large numbers of advanced strike aircraft, the Tornado IDS, from the United Kingdom. Diversity of supply decreases the likelihood that supplier nations can somehow establish a balance of military power among recipient states. If the goal of creating such a balance is to deter war, the historical record is bleak indeed; the frequency and intensity of wars in the Middle East is prima facie evidence that massive arms transfers have not led to stable political relations among states in that region.

The problem might be framed as a simple game. If a single country was the only supplier, it would be able to dictate the allocation of weapons, assuming the absence of domestic arms industries, of a significant black market, and of weapons of mass destruction. Where there are two suppliers, it is more difficult, because the second supplier can upset the balance, and intelligence about his actions is unlikely to be perfect. This is the simplified version of the U.S. versus USSR supplying arms to surrogates during the cold war. As the number of suppliers expands, including the European powers, for example, the problem increases geometrically. To the extent that supplier nations transfer arms unilaterally and in secret, which has been the historical pattern, achieving a balance becomes more difficult and fraught with complexity. And when regional powers develop military industries and acquire weapons of mass destruction, approximating real-world conditions, the value of any single transfer in promoting (or upsetting) a military balance cannot be calculated.

There are many elements working against stability in the Middle East, so much so that weapons transferred there are more likely to be used than in most other areas. It can be characterized as a highly armed region, replete with age-old religious and ethnic antagonisms, with a history of resorting to force to resolve political, territorial, and other disputes. For this reason alone, a strategy to attain stability and peace through the transfer of tens of billions of dollars in advanced fighters, tanks, anti-radiation missiles, and munitions to selected states in the Persian Gulf ought to be subject to the highest levels of scrutiny. If the past is prologue, it will continue to be very difficult to anticipate the actions of political leaders or even large-scale regime changes in the region. Under these circumstances, it is remarkable that the Bush administration so blithely announced the dual-track policy to seek multilateral restraint and then dramatically increased arms sales to the region.

This was the first American policy on arms exports that could not be buttressed by the logic of the cold war. No Soviet Union existed to arm its surrogates on the other side of an ideological divide. Indeed, arms exports from the former Soviet republics and satellite states had dropped to historic lows. There was no geostrategic need to balance armaments in the region. In the emerging world order it was important to stop Saddam in Kuwait, not for ideological reasons, but to prevent him from gaining control over the region's oil reserves and the ability to disrupt global commerce. In the wake of the Persian Gulf War, the Bush administration missed the opportunity to forge a new policy on arms exports to the Middle East. They chose instead to feed a self-perpetuating cycle, one in which the United States, the Europeans, elements of the former Soviet Union, and others export high volumes of weapons to reestablish regional balances of power upset by war or by the last round of arms sales.

The Americans and other major suppliers failed to recognize that international arms business, in which the United States is first among several prominent players, is building up a dangerously armed world. For decades, arms imported to the Middle East had raised the stakes associated with political instability and figured prominently in the calculations of militant religious regimes and regional strongmen. As the Islamic revolution in Iran has shown, once transferred, modern weapons can outlast the governments they were intended to support. As the French learned in Iraq, arms may outlast the good will of the leaders to whom they were supplied.

It is now clear what the first track of the American policy on arms exports to the Middle East involved, namely the agreement over a three-year period to sell $32.8 billion in advanced weaponry to six nations: Bahrain ($197.9 million), Egypt ($3.1 billion), Israel ($638 million), Kuwait ($3.5 billion), Saudi Arabia ($24.8 billion), and the United Arab Emirates ($593 million).[25] What of the second track, the proposal to meet with the other major suppliers and design a multilateral arms control regime for the region?

THE FIVE POWERS

The Bush announcement in May 1991 of a plan to control arms exports to the Middle East presaged a series of national and international events. Over fifty bills were introduced in the 102nd U.S. Congress that would, if enacted, have affected U.S. policies on the export of arms and military technology.[26] In June, France presented a comprehensive "Plan for Arms Control and Disarmament" to the permanent members of the UN Security Council. The French plan went well beyond the Middle East and restraint in conventional arms sales. It called upon the United Nations to endorse arms control and disarmament agreements for all categories of weapons—nuclear, biological, chemical, missiles, and conventional—and to promote the signing of regional and multilateral disarmament and

74

nonproliferation accords. For its part, France agreed, after twenty-three years of staunch opposition, to sign the NPT, as did South Africa several weeks later.[27] At about the same time, British Prime Minister John Major added his support for the establishment of an arms registry at the United Nations. And NATO reaffirmed its support for international efforts to address the problem of excessive buildup in armaments by increasing transparency and restraint in transfer policies.

Against this backdrop, the five permanent members of the UN Security Council met in Paris in July 1991 to discuss arms transfers and nonproliferation. The fact of the meeting itself seemed at odds with the arms export policies of the Bush administration. Indeed, one State Department official involved in the meetings referred to the outcome as a "public relations coup." At one level, he explained, the talks enabled Washington to assume a leadership role as a voice for restraint, but at the same time, they did not oblige Washington to moderate its arms export policies. In this aspect, the five-power talks took on the character of a public relations campaign orchestrated to appease arms control groups and critics in Congress and the media.

The international community, however, had no choice but to accept the talks for what they appeared to be—a step forward in addressing the problem of largely uncontrolled commerce in potent modern weapons. As one prominent commentator observed from Paris, "How successful this will be is not yet clear. But the fact that nations with such differing arms sales policies and international outlooks—countries that have long been in fierce competition for weapons sales—could come together is in itself striking."[28]

At the conclusion of two days of talks, the parties issued a communiqué in which they: recognized "the dangers associated with the excessive buildup of military capabilities"; agreed not to "transfer conventional weapons in circumstances which would undermine stability"; supported the establishment of an arms transfer register at the United Nations; and agreed to meet again to develop multilateral guidelines for the transfer of conventional weapons. But the communiqué also contained language to justify and legitimate the continued sale of conventional weapons to the Middle East and elsewhere. In describing the talks, it cited Article 51 of the UN Charter, which guarantees states the right of self-defense, and then extrapolated:

> That right implies that states have also the right to acquire means with which to defend themselves. In this respect, the transfer of conventional weapons, conducted in a responsible manner, should contribute to the ability of states to meet their legitimate defense, security and national sovereignty requirements and to participate effectively in collective measures requested by the United Nations for the purpose of maintaining or restoring international peace and security.[29]

The U.S. delegate to the five-power talks was none other than Undersecretary of State Bartholomew, whose views regarding arms transfers to the Middle East and elsewhere were already a matter of public record. On the first day of the talks, July 8, the Bush administration also notified Congress of its intention to make a $5-billion sale of 120 F-16 fighter aircraft to South Korea. The Korean sale included the transfer of underlying production technology, enabling the Koreans to coproduce seventy-two of the aircraft in Korea. Over the course of the next few weeks, the United States agreed to make major arms sales to Egypt, Morocco, and Saudi Arabia.

But talk of restraint nevertheless continued on the diplomatic front. The efforts of the five powers were explicitly supported later that month at the London Economic Summit by the leaders of the seven major industrial democracies (G-7), who issued a Declaration on Conventional Arms Transfers and NBC Non-Proliferation. With respect to conventional arms, the G-7 said the Persian Gulf War "showed the way in which peace and stability can be undermined when a country is able to acquire a massive arsenal that goes far beyond the needs of self defense and threatens its neighbors." They added, "We are determined to ensure such abuse should not happen again." How would that be accomplished? First, they would support the proposal to establish a universal register of arms transfers at the United Nations. Second, they would agree on a common approach to guidelines to regulate the transfer of conventional weapons, with specific reference to the guidelines under discussion in the five-power talks. Finally, they called upon all countries to "refrain from arms transfers which would be destabilizing or would exacerbate existing tensions."[30]

The Japanese delegation appears to have been a driving force behind the G-7 declaration. Their motivation, according to press reports, stemmed from intense pressure from Japanese taxpayers— each of whom had been assessed a fee of $100 to help pay for the Persian Gulf War—who felt that the war was caused by excessive arms sales to the region.[31] But the Japanese position is far deeper than the momentary pique of taxpayers would suggest. Article 9 of the Japanese constitution, the "no war clause," which was imposed on Japan by the occupation authorities after the Second World War, renounces the use of force to settle international disputes. Perhaps as a counterbalance to the heinous war crimes of their fathers, the Japanese have become a deeply pacifist people. In 1990, the Kaifu government was forced by adverse public opinion to withdraw legislation that would have permitted overseas deployment of medical and other noncombatant military personnel in peacekeeping operations under the auspices of the United Nations. As a matter of law, Japan does not export arms or military technology to other countries.[32] It is the only modern industrial nation to adopt such a position, and is therefore the only G-7 country that has not contributed directly to the arms race in the Middle East or to the overall arming of the developing world.[33]

In October, the five powers met again, this time in London. Once again, their efforts met with what appeared to be unprecedented success. They agreed to exchange information on sales to the Middle East "of tanks, armored combat vehicles, artillery, military aircraft and helicopters, naval vessels, and certain missile systems, without prejudice to existing commitments to other governments." They supported the establishment of an arms register at the UN, agreed to further talks, and most important, issued a set of "Guidelines for Conventional Arms Transfers."[34] But the progress and high-sounding language embodied in the guidelines were not matched by substance or by the subsequent actions of their architects. Indeed, the language of the October communiqué explicitly recognized the priority of "national control procedures [for] conventional arms transfers." In effect, each of the five nations would retain complete control and discretion over the decision to sell arms to countries in the Middle East. They admonished themselves not to "prolong or aggravate" existing wars, "increase tension" in the region, or "introduce destabilizing military capabilities." But they were to do so in accordance with existing national controls, the same national controls that had, in the past, resulted in a competition for sales and a continuous stream of powerful, advanced conventional weapons to the region.

On the diplomatic front, and in the eye of the public, the guidelines appeared to enunciate general principles that could, if implemented, lead to reductions in conventional arms transfers to the Middle East. They did not, however, constitute anything resembling an effective or even coherent multilateral regime that could inhibit the arms race in the region. No limits as to numbers or kinds of weapons that could be sold or otherwise transferred to the Middle East were set. No procedure enabled one nation to challenge a proposed sale of another. There were no agreed definitions, no channels for arbitration, and no verification or enforcement provisions. It was clear at the time that unless these missing elements could be added, and added quickly, disagreements over the type, volume, and destination of permissible arms transfers would erode the progress made in the first two rounds of the talks.

In the months following the July 1991 talks, the United States sold M60A3 tanks to Bahrain; Hawk antiaircraft missile upgrades and ground-based communications equipment to Egypt; F-15A/B fighter aircraft to Israel; M1 series tanks and F/A-18 fighter aircraft to Kuwait; F-16A/B fighter aircraft and military trucks to Morocco; V-300 Commando armored wheeled vehicles and missile corvettes to Oman; HMMWVs, BMY trucks, Peace Shield air defense system, MK-84 bombs, CBU-87 cluster munitions, AIM-7M Sparrow air-to-air missiles, and laser-guided bomb components to Saudi Arabia; and F-16C/D fighter aircraft to Turkey.

These sales and the avalanche of arms exports to the region that followed demonstrate that in the initial meetings of the five powers, the United States intended to leave wide latitude and discretion to the individual nations. This position was made explicit by Bartholomew on March 24, 1992, in testimony before the House Foreign Affairs Committee. He stated, "The Guidelines themselves are *not* a formula for determining who gets what. Again, we are not trying to create an international arms cartel. Rather, the Guidelines give us wide berth to question and be questioned on such matters. This is exactly what we intended when we proposed the Guidelines."[35] Bartholomew's statement was at best disingenuous, because he spearheaded an administration policy on exports which, as we shall see, ultimately abandoned the questionable yet conventional wisdom that arms sales should be instruments of foreign policy. The new policy was less about security than the expediency of electoral politics; the Bush administration tried to paint arms exports as a domestic jobs program in a desperate eleventh-hour attempt to gain electoral votes in the Midwest and California.

Throughout this period, administration officials compared the five-power talks to negotiations to reduce conventional armaments in Europe. It was not reasonable, they argued, to expect immediate results because arms control often required false steps, prolonged talks, even decades before a breakthrough could be reached; this was the lesson of the Mutual and Balanced Force Reduction (MBFR) talks, the ill-fated Conventional Arms Talks (CAT) in the Carter administration, and the Treaty on Conventional Forces in Europe (CFE) process. But the situations in Europe and in the Middle East were in no way comparable. Europe had been the center and origin of two world wars, it contained the East German–West German border and the Foulda Gap, the assumed point of confrontation between opposing forces of the West and the East, the capitalist and communist systems. But even more important, Europe was the home of numerous centers of military industry and technology; potential combatants produced their own weapons. But in the Middle East, major weapon systems could only be produced by Israel, or by Turkey and Egypt, and most of these were copies of U.S. systems like the M1 tank (Egypt) and the F-16 fighter (Turkey), made through licensed production arrangements with U.S. arms companies.

The difference was that the Middle East, like most of the rest of the developing world, was and is armed by outside powers, and so it was always possible for the several major arms suppliers to cease arming the region. As table 3.6 shows, in the last decade of the cold war, developing nations accounted for 78 percent of all arms imports but for only 10 percent of arms exports. The developed countries exported 90 percent of all weapons, but imported only 22 percent. Even after the end of the cold war, these numbers remained largely unchanged. They clearly indicate that the world arms trade is basically a transfer of weapons by a few developed nations to their less developed neighbors. In this respect, as in many others, the military sector differs from the rest of the world economy, where the vast proportion of trade and investment takes place within the developed triad of North America, Western Europe, and East Asia.

Even in 1994 and 1995, as the Israelis and Palestinians struggled to implement historic accords providing for Palestinian self-rule, high-technology arms continued to pour into the area, as if there was no relationship between the onset of war and the presence of powerful weapons on all sides. The problem, of course, was that the United States and several of the other Western powers were unwilling to sacrifice the profits of war, even in the cause of peace.[36] The only limiting factor would turn out to be worldwide recession in the early 1990s and the downward slide in world oil prices, dampening enthusiasm and slowing the pace of arms exports to the Middle East.

As to the former Soviet states and Eastern European satellites, dire economic conditions appeared to mandate the export of advanced weapons, the one industry in which the Soviets had excelled. By the end of the cold war, the Soviet Union had built up the world's largest military industrial base with an estimated three to five thousand

TABLE 3.6. WORLD ARMS TRADE: PERCENTAGE OF IMPORTS AND
EXPORTS BY DEVELOPED AND DEVELOPING NATIONS, 1981–93

Year	Imports (Developing)	Imports (Developed)	Exports (Developing)	Exports (Developed)
1981	79	21	7	93
1982	82	19	13	87
1983	79	21	9	91
1984	79	21	14	86
1985	75	25	9	91
1986	75	25	8	92
1987	79	21	10	90
1988	77	23	14	86
1989	77	24	10	90
1990	77	23	7	93
1991	74	26	9	92
1992	78	23	8	92
1993	78	22	8	92
Average 1981–85	78	22	10	90
Average 1986–90	76	23	8	92
Average 1981–90	78	23	10	90

Source: Data for the years 1983–93 are from ACDA, *World Military Expenditures and Arms Transfers, 1993–1994*, p. 91. Data for the years 1981 and 1982 are from ACDA, *World Military Expenditures and Arms Transfers, 1991–1992*, p. 89.

production facilities and a labor force of seven to ten million persons. But with the breakup of the Soviet Union, the production capability of the former republics was severely disrupted.[37]

During 1991 many Russian officials supported an aggressive arms export policy,[38] and in February 1992 Russian President Boris Yeltsin announced a policy to export Russian weapons for profit. Commenting on the decision, Andrei Kokoshin, a senior military official, stated, "If other countries would have started reducing arms deliveries, this would have had some effect, but it turned out that most democratic countries are not stopping arms sales, but increasing them. Naturally, it's very disappointing to our arms producers to see . . . other countries advancing on our markets."[39]

In late 1992, Russia agreed to sell Iran two super-silent Kilo-class diesel-powered submarines for $600 million. The first was delivered over strong protests from the United States in November 1992.[40] In addition to the submarines, Iran bought Russian MiG-29 and SU-27 fighter aircraft. At about the same time, Russia sold advanced weapons and military technology to China, including rocket engines, missile guidance technology, uranium reprocessing equipment, SU-27 fighters, and S-300 surface-to-air missiles.[41] After signing contracts to transfer about $1 billion in Russian arms to China, the two nations announced a series of agreements pledging comprehensive military and technological cooperation. When he described the accords, the Russian president said that his nation was "prepared to cooperate [with China] in all sectors, including the most sophisticated armaments and weapons."[42]

But despite these controversial sales and significant transfers of military production technology to China, the market for Russian arms did not materialize. According to the U.S. Defense Intelligence Agency:

The value of the former USSR's arms exports plummeted from a high of over $20 billion in the late 1980s to some $6 billion in 1991. In 1992, arms exports from all the former Soviet republics fell to $2.5 billion, with about $1 billion in hard currency earnings. Russia accounted for more than 90 percent of the total. Ukraine was the only other state to export major equipment, and that was in cooperation with Russia to fulfill existing Soviet contracts.[43]

It is now clear what the second, more diplomatic track of the American policy on arms exports to the Middle East involved: the espousal of high principles in multilateral negotiations without the least intention of abandoning a unilateral U.S. plan involving unprecedented growth in the U.S. share of the global arms trade. In the end, the guidelines and the five-power talks themselves were simply overwhelmed and obviated by the volume of U.S. arms sold to the Middle East. Technical talks were conducted in Washington in February 1992, which were intended to support a third round of talks at the political level that spring. But the third round did not materialize, because the arms transfer policies of the United States became transparent. On the road to achieving record levels of arms sales agreements in 1992 and 1993, the Bush administration negotiated a $6-billion sale of 150 F-16 fighter aircraft to Taiwan. In response, China suspended participation in the five-power talks, indefinitely postponing progress to control arms transfers to the Middle East.

DOMESTIC POLITICS

In the U.S. Congress, most of the significant legislative proposals to restrain U.S. (and other) arms transfers to the Middle East were combined into H.R. 2508, the International Cooperation Act of

1991. Different versions of the bill were passed by the Senate and by the House of Representatives requiring that the legislation be submitted to a conference for reconciliation. As printed in the report of the conference committee, this legislation would have committed the United States to a multilateral arms transfer and control regime, placed limits on U.S. arms transfers to the Middle East, and required the president to submit to Congress detailed reports on arms transfers to, and the military balance in, that region. But on October 30, the House of Representatives rejected the conference report by a vote of 262 to 159 and the legislation was dead.[44]

Two days earlier, however, President Bush signed P.L. 102-138, the Foreign Relations Authorization Act, which contained a section entitled "Policy on Middle East Arms Sales." It provides that the president transfer arms only to "nations that have given reliable assurances" that the weapons will be used for "legitimate" purposes. It calls upon the president to sell arms "only after it has been determined that such transfers will not contribute to an arms race" or have other undesirable consequences. Finally, it asks the president to "take steps to ensure" that recipient nations in the Middle East "affirm the right of all nations in the region to exist" and support "direct regional peace negotiations." But the "policy" contemplated by this legislation does not provide credible sanctions and is so broadly worded as to be easily circumvented by an administration intent on boosting U.S. arms exports.[45] In effect, Congress had approved the Bush administration's arms export policies because it failed to establish meaningful legislative controls.

As the U.S. presidential election of 1992 neared, the pace of politically motivated arms exports quickened.[46] In what was widely interpreted as a bid for votes in Texas, the president broke with long-standing policy: in early September he traveled to the General Dynamics

F-16 plant in Fort Worth to announce the sale of 150 F-16 fighters to Taiwan.[47]

About a week later, the president made another campaign stop at the McDonnell Douglas headquarters in St. Louis to announce the sale of seventy-two F-15 fighters to Saudi Arabia. The issue, he emphasized, was jobs, "In these times of economic transition, I want to do everything I can to keep Americans at work." The $9-billion package included forty-eight export versions of the F-15E Strike Eagle aircraft, which are capable of ground attack and can be fitted with nuclear weapons. There was immediate speculation that Israel would have to be "compensated" for the Saudi sale. Indeed, Israeli criticism of the sale was muted by promises from Washington "to provide Israel with more access to American satellite intelligence and military equipment, especially high-technology items that would enable Israel to improve its own weaponry."[48] Some observers believed that further compensation might take the form of licensed production of the McDonnell Douglas F/A-18 Hornet fighter.[49] Commenting on the sale, the Israeli Air Force chief of staff said, "There is no question that the qualitative gap between the [Saudi and Israeli] air forces has decreased."[50]

In the West, defense budget cuts in the late 1980s and early 1990s reduced the overall rate of military production. But it was a double-edged sword. Reduced procurement in the United States and Europe spurred competition for arms markets in the Middle East and East Asia, and stimulated foreign military sales from the United States. Extreme overcapacity in the military industries of North America, Europe, and Asia forced major consolidations, cross-border mergers and acquisitions, and an accelerated rate of international cooperation among companies in the production of advanced weapon systems.

These factors generated the bizarre logic that it should be the public policy of the United States to support domestic arms production by increasing exports. In the early 1990s, the United States government decided it did not need or could not afford new F-16 and F-15 fighter aircraft, M1A1 Abrams tanks, and Blackhawk helicopters, among others, but permitted such weapons to be produced solely for export markets. This was a philosophical departure from past practice in several respects. U.S. (as well as Soviet) arms transfer policies were ideologically based; cost was a second order factor, if it was considered at all. U.S. arms companies produced weapons almost exclusively for the Pentagon; they made extra copies for export, often downgraded or electronically inferior versions, ostensibly to support U.S. foreign policy goals.

But in the early 1990s, companies became more responsive to the preferences of the foreign buyers. Many more began to design weapons with foreign as well as domestic customers in mind. At the same time, elements of the Department of Defense and the State Department told Congress that even if the United States no longer needed a variety of advanced weapons, it would be possible (and desirable) to continue making them only if they could be produced for export.[51] Former Pentagon officials, now executives at McDonnell Douglas, Raytheon, General Dynamics, Hughes Aerospace, and others argued that the military industrial base must not be allowed to deteriorate, that "restarting" it would impose impossible burdens on the government. They supported increased foreign military sales as a way to "keep the base warm." Arms industry lobbyists warned of massive layoffs in congressional districts and sought to equate sales of advanced weapons to Saudi Arabia, Bahrain, Egypt, Israel, Kuwait, Morocco, Oman, Turkey, the UAE, and others with saving jobs during the recession and presidential campaign of 1992.

A particularly intense lobbying effort was mounted to support the sale of seventy-two advanced F-15E ground-attack fighter aircraft to Saudi Arabia. A coalition of U.S. arms companies and labor unions called "U.S. Jobs Now" circulated slick information packets on Capitol Hill, and played videos to interested members of Congress and their staffs. Among many inflated claims, the group argued that the F-15 sale would save forty thousand American jobs, keep the F-15 fighter production line open, perhaps into the twenty-first century, enhance U.S. influence with the Saudis, and "support peace and stability in the Middle East."[52] In a letter to then President Bush, six members of Congress endorsed these arguments and added that the F-15 sale would help balance the "unprecedented rearmament program now underway in Iran," improve the balance of trade, and "provide a bridge to other international sales," possibly to Germany. "The issue," the members pointed out, "is not whether the Saudis should buy fighter aircraft—they will do so. The issue is whether we should sell them F-15s or force them to buy additional Tornados from Britain."[53] The members' logic was not borne out; in the end, the Saudis purchased the U.S. F-15s and were reported to be buying forty-eight Tornados as well.[54]

Controversy over the sale of F-15s to Saudi Arabia was not new. In 1978, the U.S. Congress permitted the sale of sixty F-15 fighters to the Saudis, on condition that they would be stationed at a distance from Israel under a special arrangement negotiated between then Secretary of Defense Harold Brown and the Senate Foreign Relations Committee.[55] In the mid-1980s, however, no such compromise could be reached, and Congress blocked the sale of additional F-15 fighters. As a consequence, the Saudis turned to British Aerospace, the leading British arms manufacturer, and negotiated the Al Yamamah arms-for-oil deals. The two agreements, signed in 1986 and 1988, totaled between $25 and $30 billion. Due to the enormity of the sale, involving one hundred Tornado IDF aircraft, ninety Hawks, eighty helicopters, training, construction, and much more, both sides became skittish. The Saudi government was reluctant to transfer ownership of the oil to the British company, and the company was reluctant to ship weapons without payment. As the deal began to unravel in 1986, then Prime Minister Margaret Thatcher flew to Riyadh to arrange with King Fahd-Bin Abdulaziz the terms and conditions of the transfer.

The Al Yamamah deals are cited by arms industry lobbyists as evidence that unilateral attempts by the United States (or any other nation) to stem the flow of advanced weapons to developing nations will surely fail. This may be. But the proponents of global arms trading have taken this argument to dangerous extremes, and have done so in high places. They argue that in a buyers' market, another country will step in to make the sale, and therefore, because the buyer will obtain the weapons (or their equivalents), the United States government should actively promote, not restrain, the sale of U.S. arms.

This logic is usually qualified by phrases like "responsible ally," "maintain a regional military balance," and "consistent with the national security," but is nevertheless disingenuous. It simply takes the lid off by legitimating competition as the method of allocating powerful weapons—treating the arms industry as just another sector in international trade. This tendency to forget the national origins and purposes of the arms industry is a recurring theme throughout this book. For now, it is sufficient to observe that the acquisition of weapons, military technology, and an arms industry can and does change the balance of power among nations. Accordingly, nations, not companies, should set the terms and conditions of trade. Unilateral restraint by major arms-supplying nations cannot, therefore, be dismissed out of hand.

THE NEW ARMS TRADE

In the last years of the cold war, a range of technologies—civil, military, biological, nuclear, and chemical—reached maturity and were mastered by an expanding number of global industrial enterprises and nations. In tandem, Western governments generally permitted arms companies greater latitude in international sales of conventional weapons, and in developing strategic alliances and other transnational business relationships. Direct commercial sales (DCS), in which a company exports arms or transfers technology without the government acting as an intermediary, rose by a factor of eight in six years to reach $8 billion in 1988.[56] And in the first four years of the 1990s, the U.S. State Department issued an average of $26.8 billion in DCS export licenses each year. (See table 3.1, column 6.)

The change to a more aggressive arms export policy coincided with the end of a particular statesmanship associated with the logic of the cold war. As the leader of the free world, the United States made weapons available to its allies and surrogates, as grants (in the case of Israel and Egypt) and often to other nations on very easy terms. But in the absence of an ideological adversary, American largess bumped up against the ever-increasing costs of weapons and a reduced willingness of the American public to pay for them.

In the early 1990s, facing the twin challenges of intense international competition for foreign sales and reduced domestic procurement, the U.S. government took many steps to promote global sales and business operations of U.S. arms companies. State Department officials directed U.S. embassy personnel to increase the level of assistance provided to U.S. military firms, and created the Center for Defense Trade to promote U.S. arms exports.[57] In Brussels, the U.S. delegation proposed a "defense GATT" that would allow free and open trade in arms and military technology within the NATO Alliance, and with other U.S. allies.[58] The U.S. administration also proposed in March 1991 that the Export-Import Bank guarantee up to $1 billion in commercial loans to members of NATO, Australia, Japan, and Israel to purchase military equipment from U.S. companies.[59] And in early 1992, the Pentagon agreed to reimburse U.S. arms firms for their expenses in sending military hardware and personnel to weapons trade shows around the world.[60]

In his address to a joint session of Congress following the end of the Persian Gulf War, President Bush pressed Congress for greater latitude in arms transfers. "It's time," he said, "to put an end to micro-management of foreign and security assistance programs, micro-management that humiliates our friends and allies and hamstrings our diplomacy."[61] After achieving congressional acquiescence, the president used arms transfers liberally to support his policies in the Middle East, especially to reward countries that supported the U.S.-led coalition in the Persian Gulf War. In the year following the Iraqi invasion of Kuwait, the United States negotiated a record $22.5 billion in arms sales to the Middle East alone.[62]

Most important, the arms transfer policies of the United States began to look more like those of its European allies. The Bush administration proved more willing to export increasingly advanced weapons and military technologies more widely than its predecessors. And the Clinton administration not only acquiesced in the policies of its predecessor, but took steps to up the ante. In a hearing before the Senate Foreign Relations Committee in July 1993, Lynn E. Davis, the new undersecretary of state for international security, reaffirmed the Clinton administration's support for massive sales of arms to the developing world, and specifically of F-15 and F-16 fighter aircraft to Saudi Arabia and Taiwan, respectively. Davis also confirmed that Secretary of State Warren Christopher sent a cable to U.S. embassies in which he "supported both strategic trade and commercial trade on behalf of American business."[63] "Strategic trade" was, of course, a euphemism for arms exports.

In response, Senator Paul S. Sarbanes countered, "Of course, we want to encourage commercial trade as an absolute good. . . . [D]o we want to do the same thing with military goods?" Davis's answer was reminiscent of the logic, if not the cadence, that had informed the arms trade policy of the previous administration:

> I think it is more of a balancing is the way I see it, and you look at the individual cases and you look at our security and foreign policy goals and you see how they can be served at the same time by our economic goals. If they come into conflict, as they will, specific cases will almost certainly be overruled by our foreign policy goals.[64]

Davis was no novice in the field of international arms transfers. In 1977 she had worked closely, if sometimes reluctantly, in the administration of the Carter policy on arms exports, as manifested in Presidential Directive 13 (PD13). Carter had identified restraint in conventional arms transfers as a principal foreign policy objective in a speech in New York City during the 1976 presidential campaign. PD13 represented the most profound and ambitious attempt by any major power in the postwar period to stem arms exports and reduce or eliminate the trade in military technology. It is discussed in the final chapter of this book.[65]

But this enlightened policy could not withstand the test of cold war politics, and the Carter administration soon negotiated a $4.8-billion sale of sixty F-15 fighters to Saudi Arabia, seven high-technology AWACS to Iran for $1.3 billion, fifty F-5Es to Egypt, fifteen F-15s and seventy-five F-16s to Israel; the list goes on and on.[66] After an extensive analysis of the Carter policy, Andrew Pierre observed:

> Some of the administration's early statements led to exaggerated expectations. And after that, its arms transfer policy was constantly buffeted by both sides. Liberal critics saw it as a sham, a policy of exceptions, and a failure in the goal of cutting back on arms sales. More conservative observers, and those in the defense industry, viewed the policy as naive, unworkable, and hypocritical.[67]

The day following the hearing in which Senator Sarbanes had taken Davis and the Clinton administration to task, the subject of conventional arms policy was raised at the secretary's morning meeting, with Christopher, Davis, and other key players in attendance. Why, they asked, had the hearing gone so badly? The reason: they did not think it would be an adversarial proceeding and so did not prepare adequately for it. More fundamentally, there was discussion of PD13 and the Carter policy to control transfers of U.S. arms and military technology. Nobody wanted to hazard what one assistant secretary dubbed "Carter II." Because efforts to limit the arms trade were associated with a failed policy of a one-term president, Davis and her associates were unwilling to risk it again.

In the Clinton campaign there had been no steady advocate for a policy of restraint, especially because candidate Clinton endorsed controversial sales of F-15s to the Saudis and F-16s to Taiwan. After the election, when Davis and Secretary of Commerce Ronald H. Brown were installed, it was clear that arms deals negotiated by the Bush administration would go forward in a political context that placed high priority on economic competitiveness in every field, including military exports. By September of 1994 the Clinton administration had significantly liberalized export controls, for example, on dual-use computers and telecommunications equipment, and had simplified and streamlined the export administration process.[68] In what was probably a correct assessment, Brown and the Clinton White House equated decontrol of exports with increased competitiveness for U.S. companies and more jobs for Americans. The pendulum of technology controls swung from severe cold war restrictions to a wider setting.

As one arms control advocate put it in late 1993, "The United States Government, despite the holding of a presidential election more than a year ago, still does not have, as best I can tell, a considered and declared policy with respect to conventional arms transfers."[69] Instead, the Clinton administration continued along the path set by its predecessor. On September 27, 1993, Clinton issued a proclamation on nonproliferation and arms control, but it dealt only with weapons of mass destruction, and did not address the role of the United States in the global arms trade. Instead of moving forward with multilateral arms talks to control the proliferation of advanced technology weapons, the White House announced that "the U.S. will undertake a comprehensive review of conventional arms transfer policy, taking into account national security, arms control, trade, budgetary and economic competitiveness considerations."[70]

A month later, in a hearing before the House Foreign Affairs Committee, Undersecretary Davis again addressed the subject. She testified:

The review will examine the changing domestic and international arms market, the relationship among exports, jobs and the defense industrial base, and the proper role for government to play to ensure a level international playing field for U.S. defense firms. This will include the government's role in marketing, export financing, and internationalization of U.S. defense procurement.[71]

It was clear from this language that the new administration sought to craft an arms transfer policy that would give high priority to economic considerations. It heralded a policy that would, in all likelihood, be well received by U.S. military industrial interests. The "review" to which Davis had referred became known as Presidential Directive 41 (PD41) on conventional arms transfer policy.

Over the course of the next eighteen months, many agencies had a hand in crafting PD41, but principally the Departments of Defense, State, and Commerce, and the National Security Council. The Arms Control and Disarmament Agency (ACDA), which sought to install a policy of restraint, was consistently pushed to the side. In February 1995, the long-awaited policy on U.S. arms exports was issued as a classified directive. The logic for secrecy was not made clear, but from documents released by the White House, the new policy constituted a departure. It instructed senior government officials to promote the sale of U.S. weapons, and enlisted U.S. embassy personnel to that end. Further, it established "availability of comparable systems from foreign suppliers" as an important factor, and for the first time, made the economic impact on the U.S. military industrial sector a consideration in the arms transfer process.[72]

If the Clinton policy on conventional arms trade was slow in emerging from the interagency process, a series of new policies on technology transfer—the so-called Perry-Deutch initiatives—were quickly formulated at the Department of Defense. These called for the integration of civil and military technology development, reform of the Department of Defense acquisition regulations to increase access to dual-use technology and products, and for broad cooperation in the West in the development and production of military technology. As the centerpiece of the new policy regime, Secretary of Defense William J. Perry directed the military departments, the joint chiefs, and his subordinates throughout the Department of Defense to reform the acquisition process. The goal was to "increase access to commercial state-of-the-art technology" and "facilitate the adoption by [DoD] suppliers of commercial processes characteristic of world class suppliers." The plan called for "integration of commercial and military development and manufacturing" and the "greater use of performance and commercial specifications and standards" in the design and procurement of weapon systems.[73] Few observers grasped the implications that these bureaucratic initiatives held for proliferation of advanced military technology and the associated industries on a global scale. (These are addressed in chapter 5.)

4 THE SPREAD OF MILITARY INDUSTRY

BUILDING A GLOBAL INFRASTRUCTURE

At the end of the cold war, both economic and domestic political forces encouraged the melding of arms industries of different nations. In the absence of an ideological anchor, Western policy makers drifted toward the view that the armaments sector was more like other parts of the international economy than a separate element of the national security. Russian arms makers tried to compete for international sales with the West, but after a few years, several sought to establish industrial alliances with firms in the United States, in Western Europe, and in the developing world. This merely added a bizarre twist to the ongoing process of military industrial proliferation, a process that has deep roots in the postwar period. The global reach of military industry and technology can be analyzed both historically and more formally in terms of the broad array of types of collaboration in military production that emerged. Both approaches will be discussed here.

In the late 1940s, the United States held a near monopoly in the development and production of state-of-the-art weapons. It alone possessed the atomic bomb. By contrast, most military industry in Europe and Asia was exhausted or destroyed, with the partial exception of the United Kingdom. The United States emerged from the Second World War with abundant industrial, technological, labor, and natural resources. The Truman administration quickly set about converting industry to peacetime production, extending new-found wealth and largess to assist Europe, through the Marshall Plan, in economic recovery. Absolute U.S. military hegemony, however, was short-lived. The Soviet test of a thermonuclear device in 1949 shattered the hope of containing the spread of nuclear weapons technology, and the invasion of South Korea by Kim Il Sung in 1950 sullied the American vision of enduring peace. At home anticommunist ideology set the stage for the creation of an internal security state within the state that would be matched and exceeded by decades long preparation for a war in Europe that never came to pass.[1]

For the first decade following the Korean War the United States maintained unquestioned superiority in advanced military technology and industry. As the undisputed leader of the free world, the U.S. gave or sold military hardware to its allies in Europe to enhance the power of the NATO alliance, to establish rationalization, standardization, and interoperability (RSI) of weapons, and to maintain a coordinated, conventional deterrent against a Warsaw Pact invasion of Western Europe.* Although France and the United Kingdom built significant arms industries in the 1950s, there was little technical cooperation between the United States and its NATO allies. They often bought U.S. weapons, and as a consequence, a great deal of NATO military equipment initially incorporated U.S. designs. But the period of U.S. domination of European arms markets and technology ended in the early 1960s. By then, both the United Kingdom and France produced a full line of military equipment, including domestically developed combat aircraft, tanks, and battleships.

As the Europeans built up their arms industries, they became increasingly reluctant to import military equipment, and more interested in obtaining U.S. technology to make their own weapons. As one authority notes, "[L]icensed production agreements with the U.S. to build fighter [aircraft], armored personnel carriers, and helicopters were highly significant for many European defense firms. Licenses sold by the United States to countries in Europe resulted in direct market competition."[2] Like developing nations today, they hoped to use investments in military technology and complex weapons to advance the state-of-the-art in commercial industries such as civil aviation, telecommunications, computing, and electronics.

By the late 1950s and early 1960s, the United States began to transfer advanced military technology to its allies and friends, both in Europe and in Asia. As part of the effort to win the cold war, the United States entered into licensed production and other forms of technological cooperation with many armaments firms in Europe and Asia, concentrating early efforts on the former axis powers, West Germany, Italy, and Japan, whose arms industries had been

*RSI of weapons systems remains an elusive goal of the NATO alliance.

destroyed or dismantled.[3] Here American largess and ideology joined forces with the more pragmatic demands of the buyers to produce parts and components of the U.S. weapons sold to them.

But more important, licensed production of major military systems grew steadily throughout the 1960s, and by the end of the decade, over sixty major weapon systems were licensed for international production, about twenty of which were of U.S. origin. (See figure 4.3 and accompanying discussion.) The United States licensed military technology throughout the NATO Alliance, and then to its allies in Asia, principally Japan. By the mid-1970s South Korea, Taiwan, and a range of less developed nations began to produce major U.S. weapons under license. The Soviet Union licensed sophisticated military systems to China, India, and North Korea, and within the Warsaw Pact. The Europeans licensed weapons to one another, and then widely in the developing world. They collaborated to achieve economies of scale or to make a sale in lieu of geopolitical objectives.

U.S. policy makers generally viewed international armaments cooperation as a symbol of NATO Alliance cohesion and of the strength of political relations in the West. They also intended to build up the arms industries and military capabilities of the European allies. The U.S. position as a military and economic superpower meant that it could produce weapons domestically, or internationally, with little regard to cost. But from the beginning, the Europeans viewed cooperation in military technology as a way to reduce defense budgets, acquire foreign technology, employ local populations, build arms companies, and enhance economic development. The principal arms-producing nations of Europe—France, the United Kingdom, Germany, and Italy—collectively and consistently paid a substantial premium, in increased costs or decreased military performance, to produce weapon systems in Europe.

Intra-European codevelopment of weapon systems, particularly in the aerospace sector, began in earnest in the mid- to late 1960s. In 1965, France and the United Kingdom created a joint company, Sepecat, to build the Jaguar, a ground-attack aircraft which was advanced for its time. In 1968, the United Kingdom, West Germany, and Italy established two new international concerns, Panavia (for aircraft) and Turbo-Union (for engines) to build the Tornado. In 1969, France and West Germany joined together to develop the Alpha jet trainer. These early efforts to collaborate enabled the European powers to pool their military-industrial and financial resources, and to lessen their dependence on the United States for military equipment. They set the stage for the creation of a European armaments industry that by the 1980s produced military technology to rival that of the U.S. in several fields.[4]

Not only did the major arms-producing nations of Europe collaborate extensively with one another in the development and production of weapon systems, they also adopted military industrial policies in which exports have played an important role, accounting on aggregate for at least one-third of European arms production. European governments have been willing to export their most advanced weapons to a wide range of customers, several of whom have been off-limits to U.S.-based weapons manufacturers. Although they were not used effectively in the Persian Gulf War, some of the most sophisticated weapons in the Iraqi arsenal were made in France.[5] It is not unlikely that U.S. and European soldiers will again face European weapons on the battlefield, weapons that may even incorporate innovations first developed in the United States. Many transatlantic subcontracting and joint venture arrangements are now in effect. If the past is prologue, it will not be possible for the European nations and the United States to harmonize their arms export policies.

Throughout the 1980s and into the 1990s, European arms companies have been eager to exchange technology with U.S. firms, although historically, because U.S. military technology was far superior, the United States transferred a great deal more to Europe than it received. Unlike in the United States, export potential played an important role in the development of new weapon systems, and as a consequence, the Europeans proved more willing than the Americans to export state-of-the-art military equipment and technology. Accordingly, for purposes of trade and collaboration with developing countries, U.S. and European military technology and production were roughly comparable in the 1980s. Since the end of the cold war, however, the United States has upped the ante, exporting increasingly sophisticated weapons. Officials of the Department of State and Defense Security Assistance Agency (DSAA) have argued to Congress that increased foreign sales are necessary to maintain domestic production of important U.S. weapon systems.[6]

In the past, U.S. policies to transfer technology and arms to Western Europe were motivated largely by security considerations, specifically by the threat of a potential Warsaw Pact invasion of Western Europe. Those policies worked. In the space of a few decades, they helped build sophisticated arms industries across Western Europe. They also contributed to extreme peacetime overcapacity in the arms industries of the West, to intense international competition for sales of advanced weaponry, and to pressures to transfer production technology in the 1990s.

Over the next several years, it is likely that Western Europe will become increasingly self-reliant, eventually approaching security concerns not as individual nations or members of NATO, but more and more from the perspective of an independent, single European state entity. With the end of the cold war, the political forces that bound NATO together and encouraged transatlantic cooperation in military technology have already become weaker.

Differences in U.S. and European military industrial and arms export practices will figure heavily in calculating the benefits and risks associated with the Clinton administration's policies to encourage further interdependence in U.S. and European military production and technology development. (Several administration proposals are discussed in the second section of chapter 5.) In considering a U.S. policy to promote transatlantic military industrial collaboration and technology transfer, several factors will be important. Countries with whom U.S. arms makers collaborate extensively may in fact transfer weapons and technology to nations that oppose U.S. security and economic interests.

Continued transatlantic collaboration in military technology would likely increase interdependence, both in terms of shared technological benefits and risks, and with respect to production capabilities. An increase in strategic corporate alliances and subcontracting arrangements between U.S. and European arms companies indicates that this process may already be underway. Recent acquisition of U.S. arms companies by European firms, large defense cooperation staffs at the European embassies in Washington, and marketing offices of European arms firms inside the Capital Beltway also facilitate increasing European penetration of the U.S. military market.

Finally, the transatlantic exchange of weapons technology and the industrial linkages on which it depends raise additional proliferation concerns. Ultimately, nations exert very little influence over the arms export and military technology transfer policies of even their closest allies. Increasing internationalization of the military industrial base means that national controls over the distribution of weapon systems and underlying technologies become weaker. At some point in the weapons development process, technology itself becomes fungible, that is, innovations of one company working closely with another contribute to the technology base and knowledge of both. It then becomes possible for either party to build on a particular development, modify it for different applications (both military and civil), sell it in products to third parties, or transfer it as technology to others.

THE FS-X DEBACLE

In the spring of 1989, Congress debated the Bush administration's decision to help Japan develop a new advanced fighter, the FS-X, based on the F-16. Most members of Congress were unaware of the complex struggle in Japan between those who favored indigenous development of a "rising sun" fighter over a licensed production or codevelopment program with the United States. Fewer still were aware of the lobbying by McDonnell Douglas of key Bush administration officials that persuaded Washington to press Japan to buy a U.S. fighter off-the-shelf or, at a minimum, engage in licensed production of an American plane.[7]

What most understood was that a memorandum of understanding had been negotiated between the United States and Japan which called for the General Dynamics Corporation to make F-16 fighter aircraft technology available to Mitsubishi Heavy Industries, Japan's leading arms maker. This deal differed from previous military cooperation that transferred technology to Japan because—for the first time—it involved joint development of a large-scale weapon system, funded by the Japanese government, and using a Japanese company as the prime contractor. It was also different because it took place against a backdrop of trade and technology issues that continued to strain relations between the two economic superpowers.

The congressional debate over the FS-X divided the Bush administration, with the Department of Defense defending the deal against critics in Congress, the press, and the Department of Commerce. Commerce officials and others asserted that advanced technology transferred to Japan would ultimately be used to penetrate civilian aviation markets, posing a new competitive threat to the American aviation industry. They questioned whether the FS-X agreement was in the national interest, and specifically what technologies or other benefits the U.S. would receive in return. Others observed that in recent years, at the urging of the U.S. government, the Japanese military budget had risen to over $30 billion, making it roughly equal to those of the major European powers, the United Kingdom, West Germany, and France.[8] They also expressed concern that the approval to build the FS-X might constitute a step toward the remilitarization of Japan.[9]

All of this led to a fundamental misunderstanding. For their part, the Japanese negotiators considered the FS-X codevelopment project a done deal. Much political capital had been expended in the Japanese decision to abandon indigenous development of a next-generation fighter aircraft in favor of a collaboration with the United States. They were mortified when several committees of Congress revisited the terms and conditions, subjecting what had been secret negotiations to the glare of publicity and acrimonious congressional debate. By contrast, the struggle in Japan, consonant with their political system, had been conducted behind closed doors, although unsubstantiated speculation emerged from time to time in the Japanese press.

Officials of the Japanese military R&D establishment, the Technical Research and Development Institute (TRDI), who had initially planned for indigenous development of the FS-X, now hoped to use F-16 technology as the jumping-off point for the development of a superior Japanese fighter aircraft. They saw it as an opportunity to climb up the learning curve quickly, and then to experiment with military applications of new technologies developed in the commercial sector. Because the Japanese do not distinguish rigorously between military and commercial technology, Japanese industrialists also saw the FS-X as an opportunity to gain enormous technology benefits, including knowledge of systems integration, from General Dynamics. From the beginning, the Japanese approach contrasted sharply with the U.S. perspective that the new fighter would require only light modification of the F-16 design.

Proponents of the FS-X argued that advanced Japanese technology would be transferred back to the United States, including new composite wing co-curing processes and phased array radar configurations based on gallium arsenide semiconductors. In 1992, auditors for the U.S. Congress reported that General Dynamics had received "a significant level of Japanese composite wing design and manufacturing data," but that "Japan has not always been forthcoming with information pertaining to its FS-X technologies."[10] But five years after the beginning of the project, the technology benefits to General Dynamics' F-16 division (since acquired by Lockheed) and the United States government were still in doubt. Those inside Lockheed who supported the FS-X project contended that valuable composite wing technology had flowed back to the company; others were not so sure. As late as 1995, several key officials within the Pentagon remained skeptical of the value of FS-X technology, and no consensus or official position had been achieved, although a definitive study of the matter by the air force was rumored to be in the works. But what flowed back, even in the best scenario, was minuscule compared to the U.S. technology that was transferred to Japan.

In the end, the FS-X went forward, amidst rancor and controversy, but it nevertheless progressed, even though it encountered significant delays and cost-overruns, which are unusual in Japan and excruciating for Japanese officials. The debate over the FS-X fighter focused public attention on already strained U.S.-Japanese economic relations. But it largely failed to address the more immediate questions of whether or not transferring this capacity to Japan would enhance or detract from U.S., Japanese, and international security. Moreover, the fact that the FS-X codevelopment program would teach Japan to design and produce future military aircraft with far less U.S. assistance hardly registered on the political radar in Congress or the Bush administration.

Because Japan is a major export market for U.S. military technology, the FS-X codevelopment project represented a deepening of already firmly established military industrial ties. It also meant business opportunities for General Dynamics and its U.S. subcontractors; ultimately, the FS-X involved scores of subsidiary licensed production arrangements, transferring technology from U.S. to Japanese firms for major components and subsystems. As a result, the FS-X represented a significant increase in the level and sophistication of advanced military technology flowing to Japan, precisely because it involved codevelopment. It was, as Richard J. Samuels suggests, part of the larger historical process in which Japan absorbed and used U.S. military technology both as a way to rebuild its arms industries and, at the same time, as a building block and mainstay of Japanese postwar industrial and economic might.[11]

A clear progression in the structure of international cooperation in military technology can now be identified. Initially, the European powers and Japan bought U.S. military equipment through government-to-government foreign military sales programs. But while different nations pursued different strategies, and the details varied from one collaboration to the next, a pattern emerged. Each nation eventually sought to engage in licensed production or coproduction of a limited number of military items, usually because it lacked technological sophistication or could not afford to produce the system independently. Developing countries continued to buy advanced military equipment, but as time passed, they also demanded to build parts of the weapons in question, and to acquire the underlying manufacturing technology as a condition of the sale.

DEPENDENT DEVELOPMENT

In the 1980s nations of the Western Pacific sought to enhance their military power and technological prowess by tapping into military technology of foreign provenance. For many years the United States and the European powers built up the arms industries of Japan, South Korea, Taiwan, Singapore, and others through a policy of unilateral transfer of advanced military technologies, licensed production, and sale of U.S.- and European-made components and weapon systems. As a direct consequence, increasingly capable arms industries have emerged in East Asia, adding to overcapacity of production, and explicit pressure on the United States to permit the export of U.S.-designed weapon systems produced under license, particularly from South Korea.[12] In the 1990s, the nations of the Western Pacific were the only ones able and willing to maintain or increase their military expenditures; their appetite for advanced weapons and military technology seemingly whetted by the demise of bipolar East-West power relations.

Buying weapons, securing foreign military technology, and developing an indigenous arms industry often occur in parallel. Each takes place to a greater or lesser extent, depending on the level of development of a nation's arms industry and its ability to absorb and deploy new technologies. Each also represents an element in a nation's quest to augment its national security through acquisition or local production of advanced military equipment, and each has contributed to the proliferation of military industry. Compared to other global industrial sectors, in a period characterized by increasing interdependence, the arms industries maintained a higher degree of national orientation and secrecy, and were politically insulated from global economic forces.

Between 1970 and 1990 a range of developing nations achieved remarkable growth in their arms production capabilities. The expansion of the armaments industries of countries such as Israel, China, South Korea, Brazil, India, Taiwan, Australia, Indonesia, Argentina, Chile, Egypt, Pakistan, South Africa, Czechoslovakia, Greece, Poland, Spain, Turkey, and Singapore, among others, was accompanied by the increasing sophistication of their military products: fighter aircraft, tanks, armored personnel carriers, missiles, and naval craft.[13] Several developing nations entered the arms trade and were able, as table 4.1 shows, to supply a range and significant number of major weapon systems to Iraq prior to the Persian Gulf War.

The ease with which developing nations can acquire military technology and their ability to enter the arms trade has prompted one analyst to state the case in very strong terms:

The proliferation of conventional weaponry has come full circle. Conventional weapons technology has spread from North to South and is coming back around. An increasing number of the developing countries that once had little choice but to acquire their military hardware from the advanced industrial countries have taken advantage of a

TABLE 4.1. ARMS EXPORTS TO IRAQ BY SELECTED
DEVELOPING NATIONS, 1982–89

Brazil	66 Astros-II SS-30 multiple rocket launchers
	20 Astros-II SS-60 multiple rocket launchers
	13 Astros Guidance fire control radars
	200 EE-9 Cascavel armored cars
	300 EE-3 Jacara scout cars
China	4 B-6 bombers (copy of Soviet Tu-16)
	72 Hai Ying-2 ship-to-ship missiles (arming B-6 bombers)
	700 T-59 main battle tanks
	600 T-69 main battle tanks
	650 Type 531 armored personnel carriers
	720 Type 59/1 130mm towed guns
	128 C-601 anti-ship missiles
Egypt	70 F-7 fighter aircraft (Chinese version of MiG-21)
	80 EMB-312 Tucano trainers (built under Brazilian license)
	150 BM-21 122mm multiple rocket system
	100 Sakr-30 122mm multiple rocket launchers
	90 D-130 122mm towed guns
	96 D-30 122mm towed howitzer

Source: U.S. Congress, Office of Technology Assessment (OTA), from data in *World Armaments and Disarmament*, Stockholm International Peace Research Institute (SIPRI) Yearbooks (New York: Oxford University Press, 1970–90).

competitive marketplace to obtain Northern defense production technology and are now producing and exporting modern implements of warfare.[14]

Despite this perspective, and perhaps in reaction to it, the received wisdom concerning what are often called "third world" or "third tier" arms-producing nations is that they are, in fact, not very important in the overall scheme of things. The 1994 Stockholm International Peace Research Institute (SIPRI) Yearbook, a comprehensive source on armaments production and disarmament, for example, devotes scant attention to the subject, providing only one case study (of India) and one appendix. The editors conclude: "Reports that sophisticated conventional or nuclear weapons are easily or inevitably within the grasp of India, or even countries with lesser scientific resources, should therefore be viewed with skepticism." This statement is somewhat ambiguous because five developing countries with notable arms industries—India, Pakistan, China, South Africa, and Israel—are widely thought to have already produced thermonuclear devices, and in the case of Israel, both conventional and nuclear weapons would have to be considered "sophisticated."

In a separate analysis of the military industries of third tier countries, a noted SIPRI researcher suggests:

Twenty-one years ago a SIPRI study concluded that efforts to develop indigenous arms industries had not only proved very expensive but had largely failed. As the study noted, most of the countries under study had "devoted large amounts of resources to the development of weapons, particularly aircraft and missiles, which have never reached the production stage." In 1992 this conclusion remains valid.[15]

Few developing countries, according to this view, possess sufficient technology and can meet the capital requirements necessary to develop, manufacture, and support a broad range of military systems. The core of this argument is that developing countries are unable to keep up with the fast pace and evolution in state-of-the-art military technology. Although they may increase the depth and sophistication of their military technology bases and industries, they will continue to fall further behind the leaders, and possibly even the "second tier" European producers.

In one of the most interesting analyses of this subject in recent years, Ian Anthony focuses on twelve countries that have already achieved a significant level of military production, and in which "the perception that an arms industry is a strategic necessity is likely to be reinforced." These include Argentina, Brazil, Chile, Egypt, India, Indonesia, Israel, Pakistan, Singapore, South Africa, South Korea, and Taiwan.[16] This is an important sample, because it captures a great deal of the arms production activity in the developing world, even though it excludes China, Spain, Turkey, Poland, Czechoslovakia, and others. Moreover, these countries are making steady economic progress compared to many other nations, and several may be expected to join the ranks of the advanced industrial economies in the not-too-distant future.

Figure 4.1 presents an estimate of the local military production and arms imports of these twelve developing nations from 1965 through 1990 in constant 1990 dollars. There is a clear and sustained trend toward expanded local arms production over the past twenty-five years, from $229 million in 1965 to over $6 billion in 1990. Perhaps most important, after an initial decline in 1986 and 1987, arms production in these countries increased steadily for the next three years, a period when military production was declining dramatically in the United States, the former Soviet Union, and most of Europe. The level of arms imports for these countries is more volatile than their domestic production of weapons: imports fell dramatically from 1987 through 1990. Nevertheless, a second, long-term trend is clearly visible: domestic production (defined as the sum of indigenous and licensed production) tends to supplant imports. According to the estimates in figure 4.1, between 1987 and 1990 these nations cut total procurement by $7 billion (from $16.9 billion to $9.9 billion); at the same time, they increased local production from $4.7 to $6.1 billion, an increase of 30 percent.

Much of the literature that addresses arms production in the developing world assumes that developing countries seek to build up an indigenous capability that is more or less independent from the more advanced industrial nations. Building an independent arms industry may have been an ambition of some Indian leaders, particularly in the mid-1980s, and may to some extent have been forced on states like Israel and South Africa, who were subject to embargoes. But it runs counter to basic principles of the globalization of industry and of international technology transfer. Many developing nations explicitly seek foreign military technology as an alternative to importing military equipment from the major suppliers.[17]

But the paradox is that the development and production of increasingly sophisticated weapon systems is a significant drain on national technical and financial resources, especially for the less developed nations, but also for the most advanced economies. In the United States and the Soviet Union, the dissipation of competitive and productive assets increased in the 1980s and 1990s as military applications of new technologies became increasingly arcane. This was part of a decades-long process in which the center of high-technology innovation shifted to the commercial industries, and the economic benefits of technologies associated with military developments diminished.

Only in the United States (and arguably, the former Soviet Union) was it possible for a single state to make the commitment required to hold the edge in military technology. This is not now and never has been an option for the developing world. In the U.S. case, a separate military technology base of unprecedented magnitude was hived off from the rest of the economy. It consists of a vast network of laboratories and technology base programs run by the U.S. Departments of Defense and Energy, and extensive R&D and testing facilities

113

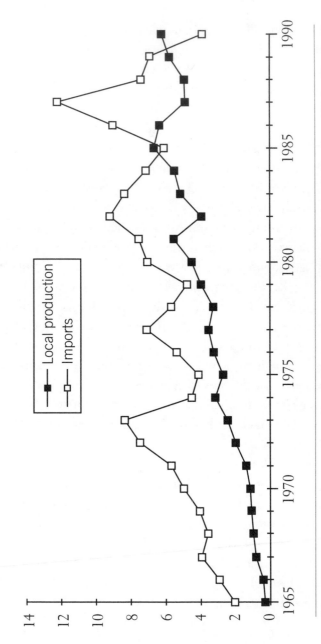

FIGURE 4.1. ESTIMATED ARMS IMPORTS AND LOCAL PRODUCTION FOR "THIRD TIER" COUNTRIES, 1965–90 ($ BILLIONS, CONSTANT 1990)

Source: Calculated using data presented in Ian Anthony, "The 'Third Tier' Countries: Production of Major Weapons," in Herbert Wulf, ed., *Arms Industry Limited* (Oxford: Oxford University Press and Stockholm International Peace Research Institute [SIPRI], 1993), pp. 370–73, table 17.1.

operated under government contracts by private sector companies.[18] The U.S. Defense Department budget for research, development, testing, and evaluation (RDT&E) has averaged over $35 billion per year for the past decade in constant 1994 dollars.[19]

In the case of the former Soviet Union, the best minds, the educational system, and the high-technology industrial infrastructure itself were oriented and subordinated to the maintenance of a military industrial complex. It can plausibly be argued that this effort undermined the Soviet economy, particularly at the end of the cold war, focusing too many assets on military activities that produced few primary or generative effects on the commercial economy. In the years following the end of the cold war, government military orders fell in Russia by over 80 percent (between 1992 and 1995), and industry collapsed throughout the former Soviet Union. Russian arms companies sought to negotiate international strategic alliances with European and American firms as a means of preserving some of their advanced technology assets.

In the United States, the final effort in the 1980s to prosecute the cold war also exerted negative although not catastrophic effects on the U.S. government and economy. Specifically, the Reagan administration decision to cut taxes and simultaneously engage in unprecedented peacetime military spending compromised the fiscal integrity of the American state. By the end of the 1980s, the American defense spend-up had wreaked havoc on the U.S. budget, institutionalizing a "state of permanent receivership," which Theodore J. Lowi had predicted a decade before.[20] When members of the American Congress turned their attention to the "peace dividend," one of the expected spoils of the cold war, all they found was deficit. The savings of lower defense spending in the late 1980s and early 1990s were simply applied to interest on the national debt. In the context of ever-increasing costs of new weapon systems, the United States canceled major programs, reduced orders for existing weapons, sought export sales to extend and preserve production facilities at home, and circled the wagons to protect the most important elements of the U.S. military technology base.

In this context, it makes little sense to suggest that developing states could construct independent military industries to supply their own needs, or expect to compete for foreign military sales, except in selected niches, and even then, probably only under exceptional circumstances. What they have done is learn to make a range of components and weapons under licensed production or other technology-sharing arrangements with firms based in more advanced economies. Success in this area would also be linked to a broader pattern of development, including a range of commercially oriented capabilities, that could then be applied to designing or building weapons on a selected basis. This is clearly a dynamic situation, closely coupled with the economic and technological power of the state. Creating a military industrial capability is not, after all, an economically rational act for any nation. Making advanced weapons at home is almost always more expensive than buying them abroad, even for the European states with advanced industrial economies, who were nevertheless compelled to collaborate among themselves to afford indigenous production.

The ability to create an arms industry depends on several conditions. First, the local industrial infrastructure must be sufficiently advanced to absorb the weapons technologies in question. Many leaders of developing countries have mistakenly believed that directing precious technical, financial, and industrial assets toward military production will automatically result in the acquisition of sophisticated commercial capabilities. Many have been sold a bill of goods by arms salesmen, who have promised more than they can deliver, both in terms of military technology, and with respect to beneficial spin-offs to the commercial sectors.

It is no coincidence that states that have made significant progress in military production also possess increasingly capable commercial industries and a rising standard of living. They are not frozen in time or permanently assigned to a particular economic tier in the international state system. That static view of the world was particularly prevalent at the height of the cold war when less developed and noncommunist states were often designated "third world," a label that tended to imply their permanent lesser status in the hierarchy of states. The recent and projected economic progress of the newly industrialized countries, especially in East Asia, is a direct consequence of their capacity to absorb and develop technology across a wide range of complex industries. What has been true of the past twenty years is unlikely to be sustained into the twenty-first century.

Building a local arms industry also depends on the availability of foreign military technology. In the 1950s and 1960s it was extremely difficult for the less developed world to absorb weapons designs and production know-how. In the 1970s and 1980s, the transfer of military technology (often in the form of licensed or coproduction) from the United States, Europe, and the Soviet Union to the less developed countries became commonplace. In the 1990s, the ability to offer sophisticated technology transfer packages to buyers in the developing world has become a salient element in the competition among firms of many nations. Within broad parameters, the buyer is able to negotiate up the technology ladder, playing one firm against another. As one authority noted, "Third World countries that want to purchase technology through licenses appear to have minimal trouble in finding multiple countries to supply them."[21]

Two points have been obscured by the increasing globalization of the arms industry. First, the decision to transfer military technology and weapons is inherently political. Historically, arms transfers were justified as instruments of foreign policy. Some observers therefore conclude that it is impossible to stop them because they are the currency of foreign relations. But it is just as reasonable to arrive at the opposite position, namely, that because the decision to sell arms involves a strong political element, political forces could be engaged to wind down the arms trade.

Second, it is manifestly impossible for a developing nation to design and produce a state-of-the-art fighter aircraft, main battle tank, or other weapons platform without significant technical assistance from foreign firms. The success of the arms industries of the developing world is predicated on their ability to acquire and absorb foreign technology.[22] If the United States and Europe stopped providing technology, the arms industries of most developing nations could not expand further and might even collapse. The corollary to this statement is, of course, that when licensing agreements and coproduction are commonplace, many nations will acquire the capability to produce military systems. The infusion of commercial technology into information-intensive weapons accelerates the process. This is elementary. But it is not yet accepted. It is the present state of play in the international state system.

Finally, the decision to build up or maintain a military industry in any nation is ultimately an act of political will. Sustaining arms production in Russia and the United States at cold war levels is impossible today in the absence of a broad political consensus that arms are necessary to protect national security. Similarly with Japan, a nation that could develop highly sophisticated weapons in any area, the political decision was made long ago to depend on the United States for military technology. With respect to the arms industries of developing nations, then, no one should be surprised that these are state-owned or highly subsidized, not unlike those of the developed world. Similarly, we should expect them to remain highly dependent on the more advanced economies for technology and even for financing, as is the case of Egypt and Israel. It is remarkable that so many developing states have made the political commitment necessary to establish and improve their arms industries. It is perhaps ironic that this process has, in recent years, been facilitated and accelerated by the political economy of the defense build-down in the United States, Western Europe, and Russia associated with the end of the cold war. It is a process which is historical and serves as a blueprint for the future.

THE REALISTS AGAIN

Even though international production of military equipment has grown continuously for more than two decades, and has accelerated dramatically in recent years, there is a persistent effort to trivialize it in the realist literature on the arms trade. This view stands in stark contrast to that of many arms industry executives in the United States. They are keenly aware of the extent of international production of weapon systems. International sales have grown dramatically as a percentage of all sales in recent years, and companies are compelled to offer licensed production and other forms of technology transfer to their customers, the vast majority of which are developing countries. The sellers are willing to negotiate because the competition for a shrinking global market is intense, and international sales are expected to reach 25 percent of their business by the late 1990s.[23]

Indeed, foreign sales are far more profitable than domestic ones. The costs of developing weapons and building initial production facilities for many major U.S. weapons were long ago passed back to the government. Weapon systems are, in fact, often taken through research, development, testing, and evaluation (RDT&E) under one set of contracts, and then re-competed when they go into production. As one company executive explained, "when foreign orders are added to an existing run for the Air Force, they are pure gravy."[24] In most cases, R&D costs are absorbed by the U.S. government with little or no funds from the company, and in cases where the company does finance R&D, it can often be reimbursed by the Pentagon under the Independent Research and Development (IRAD) program. For these reasons, a 25 percent share for foreign sales can translate into 35 to 50 percent of profits.[25] In addition, U.S. government procurement of many major systems has ended, including the M1A1 tank, the F-16, F-15, and F/A-18C/D fighters, the Blackhawk Helicopter, and the HAWK surface-to-air missile—to name a few. At the end of the cold war, U.S. arms manufacturers successfully conducted a full-court press to sell these weapons abroad. Licensed production was often a major element of the sale.

Despite these circumstances, realist writers such as Neuman (in 1984) and Krause (in 1992) have sought to minimize the importance of the arms production capabilities of developing states.[26] Neuman in particular acknowledges that licensed production and other forms of commerce in advanced military technologies holds the potential to change the complexion of the arms trade and the stakes for various nations:

Since the late 1970s, the character of the world arms trade has been changing. Technology, not military end-items, has become the new medium of exchange. As the transfer of technical data and industrial know-how has increased in proportion to the sale of finished systems, new arms production facilities have appeared, particularly in the Third World, throwing traditional supplier-recipient relations into flux.[27]

But having said as much, she is then at great pains to downplay the contribution that developing states make to arms production. By her count, the number of developing states producing arms grew from four in 1950 to twenty-seven in 1980, a considerable increase, but then she says it leveled off between 1980 and 1984.[28] Again by her count, the number of major weapons produced under international licensing agreements rose from 10 in 1950 to 178 in 1980, a dramatic escalation, but most of them, she says, were accounted for by only a few countries. Moreover, the weapons are inferior. Developing countries "produce fewer, older, and less complex defense items" than the most advanced nations. Finally, she notes, only six of the developing states produced a full range of major weapons platforms. The intent of this analysis is to write off the arms production capability of the developing states, to relegate it to an insignificant "tier" in a hierarchically structured "global defense production system." The "system" essentially mirrors the overall structure of bipolar power relations within the international state system.

The tendency to dismiss the arms industries of the developing world as technologically primitive, and to pigeonhole them as a lower tier in a highly stratified global arms production system, is not merely an artifact of the cold war. Contemporary analyses also use this device to impose order on an otherwise rather messy and interconnected web of arms producers based in different nations. One recent account describes a multitier arms production trade system, comprised of five ideal types: first, second, and third tier suppliers and strong and weak customers. These correspond to four levels in a technology hierarchy, with the weak customers unable even to operate the weapons they have bought. In this view "third tier suppliers copy and reproduce existing technologies (via transfer of design), but do not capture the underlying process of innovation or adaptation."[29]

Written eight years after Neuman, and with the benefit of hindsight, Krause's analysis is strikingly similar to the point of reiterating most of the arguments made in Neuman's 1984 article. He acknowledges a "great expansion" in the number of producer states, but notes that their weapons are based on "first-generation post-1945 technologies." (Clearly there are exceptions such as the M1A1 tank, licensed to Egypt; the F-16 fighter, licensed to Turkey and South Korea; the German Type 209 submarine, licensed to Brazil and South Korea; and the Soviet MiG-27, licensed to India.) Even though they are able to produce sophisticated weapons, third tier arms producing countries are "restricted to only one or two weapons systems." In addition, although they may produce and export more weapons than they used to, "third-tier producers have neither successfully freed themselves from dependence upon imported components nor captured the process of technological innovation." In the end Krause, like Neuman, "confirms the hierarchical and stratified structure of global arms production," suggesting that further growth in the number of producers is unlikely, as is growth in their share of global arms production and trade.[30]

A number of assumptions that buttress this line of argument have been weakened or obviated by the end of the cold war. The first is that the world is frozen in a set of fundamental relationships. States may increase or decrease their power at the margins, arms production may rise and fall, but the relative levels of both state power and arms production are fixed within established tolerances. These tolerances are defined by the ideological contours of the cold-war confrontation between capitalism and communism. A second assumption is that because of this confrontation, armaments production will continue to increase. Developing countries may create more weapons, but they are unlikely to increase their share of global arms production because it is an ever-expanding pie. In this view, the arms industries of the developing world are seen as a manageable consequence of superpower competition. A third assumption is that the economic organization of states essentially reflects their political orientation. Hence we have the first world of modern industrial democracies led by the United States, the second world of communist states tied to the Soviet Union, and the third world of developing states of indeterminate political persuasion. In this essentially static hierarchy, the principal elements of commerce—capital, technology, trade, investment, communications, and business organization—cannot cross over political barriers, except with the greatest difficulty.

As the international state system came unglued, and the Soviet Union dissolved, the weapons production capacity of the Warsaw Pact diminished significantly. It is doubtful whether Russia today is still in a class with the United States as regards the design and manufacture of many next-generation weapon systems. Indeed, in five years' time, it is likely that combined Western European production of arms may exceed that of the former Soviet Union, with respect to both quantity and quality. This circumstance alone enhances the importance of the arms industries of the developing world. Moreover, because the Soviet Union no longer exists to supply free weapons to its clients, nations that depended on the Soviets may take steps to find new sources of supply or to increase local production, or both.

The end of the cold war also undermined the assumption that arms production will continue to increase. Indeed, everywhere except for the developing world, domestic arms production is decreasing. The developing world has been able to increase its production by substituting licensed and coproduction arrangements for imports of weapon systems. A smaller pie means increased competition for shrinking global markets, but it also ensures that in the absence of government action to forestall it, technology will increasingly become a major currency of the arms trade. In the aftermath, it is difficult to see how political leaders came to accept as legitimate the monumental levels of weapons production embedded in all of this. It is a kind of self-fulfilling prophecy. If international relations is really only about power, as the realists suppose that it is, and not about mutually beneficial economic cooperation, then it is necessary to prepare for war at all levels in the international state system. Never mind that preparations for war on a grand scale litter the world with potent weapons and the industries that produce them. The expansion of the pie appears, under realist assumptions, to be a natural and even reasonable outcome.

Finally, the assumption that states are somehow fixed in a hierarchy, because of either their political orientation or economic status, has been weakened on at least two counts. First, some former communist states may succeed in establishing democratic institutions and efficient market mechanisms. And second, several states that were classified as developing nations ten years ago have achieved advanced technology, capable industrial infrastructures, and increasingly high standards of living for their populations. Why should they be less successful in building weapons industries than they are in a wide range of commercial high-technology sectors?

To the contrary, there is every reason to expect that they will continue to infuse increasingly sophisticated commercial technology into weapons programs. Embedded in the realist pessimism over the so-called third world arms industries is a theory of development that sees a persistent stratification among industries of different nations. It views developing nations as structurally prohibited from achieving technological and industrial accomplishments commensurate with those of the advanced industrial democracies. It is defeated by pervasive and compelling evidence of multinational production of advanced weapon systems. The remarkable economic progress of a range of East Asian nations, and incidentally, the persistence of their arms industries, also belies this basic assumption. It will not be long before the realist writers assert that disarmament is impossible precisely because the developing nations have somehow managed to master the fundamentals in a range of military industrial sectors.

COMMERCE IN MILITARY TECHNOLOGY

In the mid-1990s, the United States was the only country that could hope to stay at the forefront in the development and production of all major kinds of weapon systems. The individual nations of Europe had long since reached the limits of national military production and found ways to circumvent them. Such limitations were also evident in Russia and the other former Soviet republics, and increasingly so, as the Soviet military industrial complex collapsed. The dependence of Europe, Russia, and a range of developing nations on international collaboration to develop and build new weapons reflects an increasingly global texture of commerce in military technology "in which transnational technology transfers take place either within multinational corporations or between teams of companies."[31] The emergence of large-scale weapons firms that can transfer technology and manufacture weapons in several different nations signals the disengagement of the nation-state from weapons design, development, production, and, ultimately, control.

This evolution is partly a consequence of a notable shift in the economic power surrounding weapons sales from the seller to the buyer. For a quarter century following the Second World War, the terms under which foreign military transfers were conducted, and the extent to which weapons technology was shifted from one nation to another, were the province of the seller. In the U.S. case, the authority of the seller was vested in the Departments of State and Defense. But in recent years, as several prominent analysts have recognized, buyers call the shots. Technology transfer and countertrade have become standard elements of the transaction, and decisions regarding the exchange of technology have increasingly been delegated from organs of the national state to private sector producers of military material.

The assumption of authority concerning the diffusion of military technology by the private sector is also partly a function of the increasing dual-use character of technology development and corresponding changes in the structure of international business. From 1987 to 1992, the amount of global foreign direct investment (FDI) doubled from $1,000 billion to $1,949 billion.[32] While there are many measures of FDI, and economists disagree on what they mean, one point is not disputed: over the past decade, cross-border investment by multinational corporations has transformed the international economy, vitally affecting trade and the transfer of technology on a global basis.[33]

Although the arms companies have tended to maintain their national orientations longer than firms in other sectors, they have not been immune to the forces of global economic integration. Indeed, large-scale arms companies in the U.S. and Europe have consolidated their operations, merged or acquired other firms to achieve scale economies, and sought to extend their marketing, sales, production, and service operations to other nations. In this respect, they appear to be following a course not dissimilar to that pursued by multinational corporations in the commercial industries twenty-five years ago.

There is, of course, a continued political component to the decision to sell arms and military technology to foreign firms. But such transfers must be distinguished from multinational arms production and from cross-border mergers and acquisitions, which have grown to encompass many aspects of weapons design and production. This can be traced along several dimensions. First, twenty-five years ago, there was little international production of major arms. Now it is commonplace. Second, until recent years, especially in the United States, development and production of weapon systems was closely controlled by military specifications, Department of Defense standards, and the defense acquisition regulations (DFAR). Intense regulation made it difficult for Department of Defense contractors to draw efficiently on the commercial economy. It also discouraged mergers with or acquisition of commercial companies by arms firms and vice versa, and in cases where mergers and acquisitions (M&As) did occur, elaborate administrative arrangements were often implemented to separate military from civilian technology development.

In the years leading up to the end of the cold war, and in its aftermath, integration of civil and military production, even in the

United States, increased at the level of the firm. This trend is being driven by the perceived need for greater efficiency in military production, in relation both to smaller arms markets globally, and to escalating costs of developing modern weapons. In Europe, civil-military integration has historically been more advanced than in the United States, largely because defense budgets and production runs were too small to tolerate inefficiencies associated with dedicated military R&D and production. In the Japanese case, no dual-use distinction is made; each commercial or military product is simply one more application derived from a common base technology.

Nevertheless, as U.S. policies on arms acquisition, global arms sales, and international transfer of military technology come to resemble those of Europe more closely, continued integration of civil and military technology constitutes yet another vehicle for the proliferation of weapons and the industrial enterprises that produce them. The overall effect of infusion of civil technology into military production, and the multinational development, production, and marketing of new weapon systems, has yet to be understood fully. Increasing efficiency at the level of the firm, and achieving new budgetary and technological synergies in military procurement, may make U.S. military equipment more affordable than it otherwise might have been. But there will also be unintended consequences. These include a systematic increase in the proliferation of powerful weapons and military technology, as well as the international industrial infrastructure that supports production.

Collaboration in the development and production of military technology and systems is an extremely complex enterprise, and it takes many different forms. It can be conducted among governments or in the private sector or some combination of the two. Collaboration is actually a catch-all term encompassing a wide range of administrative, financial, political, and industrial relationships. It can be limited to international exchange of data or of scientists and engineers among government laboratories and public or private sector arms firms. It can also refer to licensed production or coproduction, codevelopment, security assistance, direct commercial sales, joint ventures, and a wide variety of other institutional and political mechanisms. Some arrangements are open-ended; others are highly delimited.

Table 4.2 presents the principal forms of international collaboration in military technology. They are arranged roughly in ascending order, according to their potential to transfer technology from one nation to another. The table is noteworthy in two respects. First, it is striking the extent to which these forms of international military collaboration mirror what has gone on before in the private sector. Many collaborations in military technology are, in fact, typical of those found in multinational commerce across the range of commercial sectors. Although the development of fully multinational arms companies is an evolving phenomenon, arms firms of different nations have adopted many of the organizational structures and business practices that define multinational corporate enterprise generally.

Second, as the data illustrate, over the past decade there has been a strong trend away from government-to-government cooperation toward more technologically intensive interaction among arms firms based in different nations. As the industrial infrastructure for international production of weapons has expanded over time, government-led programs have been pushed to the margins. Large-scale arms companies are increasingly entering into cross-border acquisitions, joint ventures, and other forms of industrial cooperation. In the transatlantic context, for example, cooperation between U.S. and European companies increased dramatically in the late 1980s, including such mundane-sounding deals as the Westinghouse-Plessey missile

TABLE 4.2. FORMS OF INTERNATIONAL
MILITARY INDUSTRIAL COOPERATION

Sourcing   Direct purchase of foreign-made parts and/or components for weapons systems.
Examples: Use of Japanese ceramic packages, computer chips and flat panel displays, all dual-use items, in U.S. military systems. Offsets in the F-16 program where foreign parts and components are used to produce aircraft in Fort Worth, Texas.

Subcontracts   A company in one nation lets a contract with a firm of another nation to develop or produce a portion of a weapon system for which it holds the initial or "prime" contract.
Examples: Martin Marietta's subcontracting to Rafael (Israel) in the Popeye standoff missile. South Korean production of Dornier 328 fuselages for DASA (Germany). F-16 program.

Risk Sharing   International business activity where each company invests in its area(s) of competence with agreement to share benefits/risks.
Examples: Partnerships by European aerospace firms in the Argentine-Brazilian CBA-123 transport plane. Also, partnerships by Portugal in the Belgian Promavia Jet Squalus trainer jet.

Licensed Assembly   Assembly under license of the parts and components of a weapon system supplied by another country.
Examples: U.S. M1A1 tank (by Egypt), U.S. F-5 fighter (by Taiwan), Korean F-16 initial run (later production will be licensed production).

Technology Transfer   International exchange of technical staff and of technological specifications. Also licensing of military technology.
Examples: Hundreds of military data exchange agreements (DEAs) between U.S. DoD and its counterparts in other nations. U.S. "swing-wing" technology to Tornado program, German design and systems integration assistance on the Argentine IA-Pampa trainer jet (DASA), French design assistance on Indian Light Combat Aircraft (LCA) program, technical data packages (TDPs) provided by U.S. to Taiwan for the indigenous design and production of artillery pieces.

Licensed/Coproduction   Production under license in one country of a part, component, or weapon system originally developed in another country; joint production of a part, component, or entire weapon system by firms of different nations.
Examples: The U.S. F-15 and numerous other systems (to Japan), the U.S. M1A1 Abrams tank (to Egypt), the U.S. F-16 fighter and Multiple Launch System (to Turkey), the German Type 209 submarine (to Brazil and South

TABLE 4.2. *(continued)*

Korea), the French Alpha Jet (to Egypt), the Soviet MiG-27 fighter and T-72 tank (to India), the U.K. Swingfire Anti-Tank Missile (to Egypt), the French Super Puma helicopter (to Indonesia), the French Milan Anti-Tank Missile (to India), the German BK 117 helicopter (to Indonesia).

Tactical Alliances   (Sometimes called "strategic" alliances.) Loose agreements among firms to collaborate in specific areas of development and/or production of military technology and weapon systems.
   Examples: General Dynamics and British Aerospace on armored vehicles. British Aerospace and Dassault on combat aircraft.

"Family of Weapons"   An international division of labor involving several related weapon systems; participating countries separately develop a particular weapon within the group and then permit the other participants to produce that weapon for themselves, used by NATO.
   Examples: AMRAAM/ASRAAM.

"Nunn Amendment"   Government-to-government programs for joint development of common weapon systems.
   Examples: NATO Frigate Replacement (NFR90), Modular Stand Off Weapon (MSOW), and NATO Anti-Air Warfare Systems (NAAWS). Most failed because it was too difficult to harmonize military requirements, too much regulation, and the systems tended not to be central to the needs of the participating armed services.

Codevelopment/Teaming   Joint development (research, design, and/or engineering) of a part, component, or entire weapon system by firms of different nations, often involving a prime contractor-subcontractor relationship.
   Examples: European Fighter Aircraft. Anglo-German-Italian Tornado fighter, Franco-German HOT/Milan antitank weapon, U.S.-British AV-8B fighter, Franco-German APACHE standoff weapon, U.S.-German-French-Italian Medium-range Extended Air Defense System (MEADS).

Joint Ventures   A jointly owned corporate entity to pursue the development and/or production of a particular military technology or weapon system.
   Examples: Franco-German "Eurocopter" (Aerospatiale and DASA), Anglo-French missile JV (British Aerospace and Matra), U.S.-French jet engine "CFM International" (GE and Snecma), Anglo-French missile JV "Thomson-Shorts" (Thomson-CSF and Short Brothers). Franco-Italian software for missiles "Eisys" (Elettronica and Syseca). U.S.-German jet engine "CSC" (MTU and Pratt & Whitney).

TABLE 4.2. *(continued)*

Consortia   Agreement of several partners to pursue a technology area or weapon system from shared resources with shared revenues.
Examples: Panavia which produces the Tornado fighter-bomber. Eurofighter is developing the European Fighter Aircraft.

Mergers & Acquisitions   The purchase or exchange of equity by arms firms of different nations, including outright purchases of a firm.
Examples: Thomson-CSF (France) took over HSA (Netherlands), DASA (Germany) took over Fokker (Netherlands), GM Hughes (U.S.) took over Rediffusion (U.K.), Matra (France) took over Fairchild (U.S.), Snecma (France) took over FN-Moteurs (Belgium).

"Circle of Friends"   Loose concept floated by the Clinton administration to encourage broad-based international cooperation in military technology.

---

approach warning system, the Atlantic Research–British Aerospace missile propulsion system, the Lockheed-Sanders-GEC Osprey ASW sonar, the Boeing-Thomson SDI free electron laser, the GE-GEC Ruston T-700 Blackhawk engine, the Thiokol–British Aerospace rocket propellant, and scores of others.

Increasingly, the transfer of military technology from one nation to another takes the form of private business deals, which must be approved by governments but are otherwise conducted outside official channels. Intense competition for shrinking markets, for both weapons and military technology, is driving globalization. At the same time, it is weakening the role of the nation-state, with the result that the determined buyer can almost always acquire the desired weapons and military technology or the rough equivalent from one supplier or another.

The shift from public to private sector international collaboration in military technology and arms production is clearly visible in data collected by the Defense Budget Project (DBP), a Washington-based think tank. The DBP Globalization database documents over five hundred cases of international collaboration among arms firms dating from the early 1960s. It includes instances of international consortia, teaming arrangements, joint ventures, mergers, acquisitions, and strategic alliances that were established to develop and/or produce a major weapon system or important component. These data do not include instances of licensed production such as the U.S. F/A-18 fighter licenses with Finland and Switzerland or the Russian MiG-29 fighter licenses with India and North Korea.

Figure 4.2 shows the number of international weapons programs started during each five-year period from 1961–65 through 1991–95 (estimated). There are two notable trends. The first has to do with the dramatic rise in collaborative programs in recent years. In the 1960s and 1970s, there were twenty-five or fewer new start-ups for each five-year period. But in the years 1981–85, that number more than doubled to sixty, and in the next ten years, it mushroomed to over two hundred new weapons programs. Analysis of these data suggests that about three-quarters of international collaboration is accounted for by intra-European and transatlantic cooperation, and about one-quarter is shared among Europe-Asia, U.S.-Asia, intra-Asia, and other arrangements.[34]

The second major trend shown in figure 4.2 is that until the mid 1980s, government-led projects dominated international collaboration, but after 1985, they were rendered insignificant in comparison to private sector activity and actually declined. These data indicate that the globalization of military industrial activity is a relatively new phenomenon, manifesting itself on a large scale only over the past ten years. The surge in the international commercialization of arms industry and technology clearly predates the end of the cold war, indicating that it is probably less driven by geopolitical factors than by transnational maturation of the global arms industrial enterprise.

The fact that international collaboration has continued to increase in the post–cold war period, even as world arms production shrinks, suggests that it is well established as a modality of production and is contributing to the proliferation of increasingly sophisticated weapons and the production processes associated with them.

Industrial linkages between U.S. arms companies and weapons producers in the developing world have also expanded in recent years. These are frequently built into the structure of arms sales. What used to be straightforward sales of major platforms have now become sales combined with eventual licensed production of all or part of the component or weapon in question. These kinds of arrangements also contribute to globalization of the military industrial base. Global sourcing may already be making arms production more efficient, but in the long term, it will also tend to displace U.S. military subcontractors (and U.S. workers) and increase U.S. dependence on foreign-made weapons.

THE CASE OF LICENSED PRODUCTION

Most discussions of international commerce in military technology focus on one kind of technology transfer, that is, licensed production of major military systems. The findings of one extensive survey of licensing were summarized as follows:

> First, technology is transferred through licensed production by a large number of countries. Second, there are only minor differences between the pattern of licenses supplied to Third World and to developed countries. Third, suppliers are in as vigorous competition to provide licenses as they are to export arms. And, fourth, Third World countries that want to purchase technology through licenses appear to have minimal trouble in finding multiple countries to supply them.[35]

FIGURE 4.2. GROWTH IN INDUSTRY-LED INTERNATIONAL COLLABORATION, 1961–95(E)

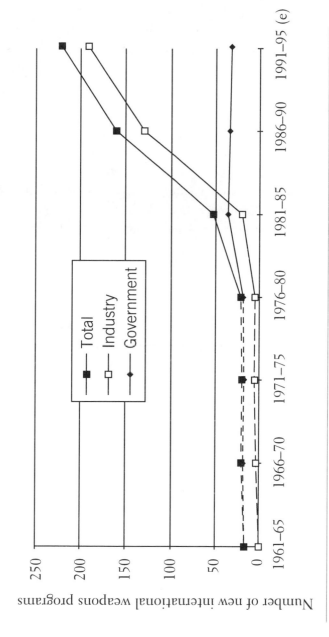

Source: Defense Budget Project, *Database on International Collaboration in Military Production* (Washington, D.C.: Defense Budget Project, 1995).

These results are extremely important because they indicate not only the pervasive nature of licensing, but also that, for purposes of the arms trade, the distinction between technology and finished weapons has diminished significantly. Technology transfer is no longer just an add-on to close a major sale, it has become an object of competition itself.

Licensing of major weapon systems constitutes a principal means of communicating technology across national borders, but it is only a part, and perhaps not the greatest part, of a broader picture. Moreover, any study of licensing activity at the level of the major weapon system grossly understates the magnitude of technology transfer and the complexity of the international military industrial relationships that have developed.[36] An overall license may be issued by one company to another for any given weapon system, but there will always be additional or subsidiary licenses for major parts and components. These can be quite extensive. The U.S. transfer of F-15 fighter production technology to Japan, the F-15J program, provides an apt example. In studies that total up licensed production, the F-15J fighter is usually counted as one major military system. The impression given by this method, however, misrepresents the magnitude of what is going on.

In the first place, the F-15J program is an enabling activity because it transfers to Japan systems integration technology without which Japan could not possibly have built such an advanced fighter aircraft. Second, the F-15J program is an umbrella organization under which a great many U.S. and Japanese companies are engaged in producing and even developing a large number of diverse military products. Most of the Japanese firms involved already possess highly sophisticated military and civil technological capabilities. Table 4.3 suggests the volume and character of the technology transferred to

Japanese firms under this program. There are at least fifty separate licenses which involve close collaboration among Japanese and U.S. firms across a very broad range of technologies.

Third, most of the Japanese companies engaged in licensed production of F-15J components are in fact primarily oriented toward nonmilitary commerce. Most Japanese firms listed in table 4.3 are highly adept at absorbing technology in one area and then developing it for future applications in another. Once they have mastered the particular military application for which the license was issued, they are often able to modify it, and apply it to a range of new products, both military and civil. There is, accordingly, a secondary commercial incentive at the level of the firm to engage in licensed production of military components.

Even though the data on licensing of major military systems are inadequate and significantly understate the international, organizational, and technological relationships involved, they depict basic trends and the extensive nature of international commerce in military technology. A 1991 study by the Office of Technology Assessment (OTA) examined several facets of licensed production. Figure 4.3 shows the growth of worldwide licensed production of major weapon systems, including those licensed to other countries by the United States.* The figure shows that in 1960, licensed production of major weapons was negligible, but increased steadily throughout the 1960s

---

*Figure 4.3 shows a leveling off and slight decline in the number of major weapon systems produced under license, both worldwide and for U.S.-origin equipment. This is due in part to the twelve-year production cycle (assumed in the figure) and partly because the number of new systems licensed is relatively constant throughout the seventies and eighties. However, 1988 (the last year for which data are provided) saw the largest number of new systems licensed and the greatest increase in the number of new license agreements for U.S.-origin equipment.

TABLE 4.3. SELECTED F-15J SYSTEMS/COMPONENTS LICENSES

System/Component	Licensee	Licensor
Fire control	Mitsubishi Electric	Hughes
Radar display	Tokyo Instruments	Sperry
Data link recorder	Hitachi	McD. Douglas
UHF radia	Mitsubishi Electric	Magnavox
Head-up display	Shimadzu, NEC	McD. Douglas
Lead computing gyro	Toshiba	GE
Inertial navigation	Toshiba	Litton
Autonavigation	Mitsubishi Electric	Rockwell Collins
Identify friend/foe	Toyo Commun. Equip.	Hazeltine
Identify friend/foe	Toyo Commun. Equip.	Teledyne
Aircraft assemblies	Daicel	McD. Douglas
Sidewinder power	Nippon Aircraft	West Electronics
Simulators	Mitsubishi Precision	Goodyear Aero
Engine parts	IHI	Bendix
Elec-chem. machined parts	IHI	TRW
Magnetic detection	Mitsubishi Electric	Texas Instruments
Dopler navigation	Mitsubishi Heavy	Teledyne/Ryan
Automatic flight control	Kato Aircraft Instr.	Lear Siegler
Encryption	IBM Japan	IBM
Flight computers	Japan Avionics Electronics	Honeywell
Engine parts	Eagle Industries	EG&G
Overspeed detection	Shimadzu	McD. Douglas
Air inlet controller	Hokushin Electric	United Tech.
Forward engine ducts	IHI	Rohr
Indicators	Tokyo Instrument	Ragen Data Systems
Airfoils	Nittaku Metal	TRW
Horiz. situat. indic.	Tokyo Aircraft Instr.	Rockwell
Fuel tank	Shin Meiwa	Sargent-Fletcher
Fuel pumps	MHI	TRW
Transceivers	Hokushin Electric	Bendix
Wheel/brake components	Kayaba Industries	Bendex
Engine manifold	IHI	Ex-Cell-O
Filtration equipment	Kaikin Kogyo	Aircraft Porous Media
Stretched acrylic sheet	Mitsubishi Rayon	Sweedflow
Engine temp. indicator	Tokyo Aircraft Instr.	Gulf Airborne
Evan history recorder	Shinko Electric	Teledyne
Radar warning	Tokyo Instruments	Itek
Control stick compensator	MHI	Moog

TABLE 4.3. *(continued)*

System/Component	Licensee	Licensor
Interference blanker	Mitsubishi Precision	McD. Douglas
Munitions handling	Nittoku Metal	GE
Stabilator	MHI	Pneumo Corp.
Aileron	Sumitomo Precision	Pneumo Corp.
Nose steer/flap drive	Teijin Seiki	Pneumo Corp.
Hydraulic valves	Teijin Seiki	Parker-Hannifin
Fire control	Shinko Electric	Dynamic Control
Pneumatic and fuel ducts	Yokohama Rubber	Goodyear
Pneumatic and fuel valves	Teijin Seiki	Sunstrand
Fuel tank	Yokohama Rubber	Goodyear
Electic generator	Shinko Electric	Lear Siegler
Landing gear	Shinko Electric	McD. Douglas

Source: Richard J. Samuels, *"Rich Nation, Strong Army": National Security and the Technological Transformation of Japan* (Ithaca, N.Y.: Cornell University Press, 1994), p. 232, table 7.3.

and 1970s. By 1980 and in all subsequent periods, approximately 180 major weapon systems were being produced under licenses.

One of the 180 was the F-15J fighter. Among many other examples, the United States transferred highly advanced production technology for the Stinger missile to Germany, Belgium, Greece, Italy, the Netherlands, and Turkey; for the Patriot Air Defense System to Japan and Italy; and for the AIM-9L Sidewinder air-to-air missile to Japan, Germany, Norway, Italy, and Taiwan. These agreements often included direct offset provisions, in which production technology is transferred to a foreign firm with the understanding that the buyer will produce a given component for all subsequent copies of the weapon, even if the system was made in the U.S. and sold to the Pentagon. In the F-16 fighter program, for example, production technology was transferred to Denmark, Belgium, the Netherlands,

FIGURE 4.3. ESTIMATED WORLDWIDE LICENSED PRODUCTION OF
MAJOR CONVENTIONAL WEAPON SYSTEMS, 1960–88

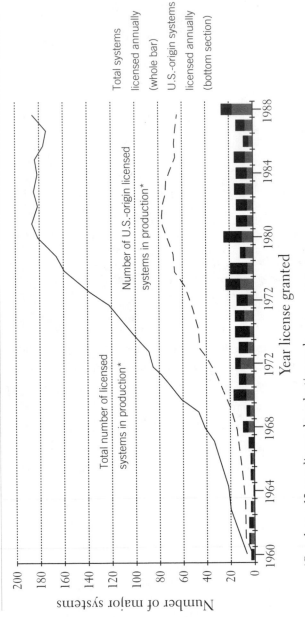

Year license granted

Number of major systems

Total systems licensed annually (whole bar)

U.S.-origin systems licensed annually (bottom section)

Total number of licensed systems in production*

Number of U.S.-origin licensed systems in production*

*Based on a 12-year licensed production cycle.

Source: U.S. Congress, Office of Technology Assessment (OTA), *Global Arms Trade: Commerce in Advanced Military Technology and Weapons*, OTA-ISC-460 (Washington, D.C.: U.S. Government Printing Office, June 1991), p. 7, fig. 1.7.

Norway, and much later to Turkey and South Korea. Components of aircraft assembled in Fort Worth, Texas, are made in many countries of the world.[37]

The OTA report also shows the extent to which the United States, Europe, and the former Soviet Union transferred advanced military technology to less developed nations. In 1988, for example, India, Egypt, Indonesia, South Korea, Taiwan, and Brazil were producing forty-three different major weapons under international licensing agreements. Major systems transferred have included the U.S. M1 Abrams tank (to Egypt), the U.S. F-16 fighter and Multiple Launch Rocket System (to Turkey), the German Type 209 submarine (to Brazil and South Korea), the French Alpha Jet (to Egypt), the Soviet MiG-27 fighter (to India), the British Jaguar fighter (to India), the French Super Puma helicopter (to Indonesia), the French Milan Antitank Missile (to India), and the German BK 117 helicopter (to Indonesia), among others.[38]

The pattern in the growth of licensed production by developing nations followed the overall trend closely. Figure 4.4 shows that in 1960, only two major weapon systems were being produced under license in the developing world. By 1980, that number had grown to ninety, representing about half of all licensed production of major military systems. The United States has taken the lead in transferring military technology, issuing about as many licensed production agreements as the former Soviet Union and the European NATO powers combined. Table 4.4 suggests the extent of licensing arrangements between the United States and two newly industrialized countries, South Korea and Taiwan.

The Defense Budget Project also maintains a database on licensed production, which is distinct from the cases of international collaboration in military technology described in figure 4.2. The DBP

TABLE 4.4. SELECTED MAJOR U.S. WEAPON SYSTEMS PRODUCED UNDER LICENSE BY SOUTH KOREA AND TAIWAN

South Korea
F-16 Fighting Falcon fighter
F-5E Tiger-2 fighter
F-5F Tiger-2 fighter
H-76 Eagle helicopter
Model 500MD helicopter
PL-2 light plane trainer
M-101-A1 105mm towed howitzer
M-109-A2 155mm self-propelled howitzer
M-114-A1 towed howitzer
CPIC type fast attack craft
LCU-1610 type landing craft
PSMM-5 type fast attack craft

Taiwan
F-5E Tiger-2 fighter
F-5F Tiger-2 fighter
F-5F Tiger-2 trainer
Model 205 UH-1H helicopter
AIM-9J air-to-air missile
AIM-9L air-to-air missile
MIM-23B Hawk land mobile surface-to-air missile
M-60-H main battle tank
FFG-7 class frigate
PL-1B Chienshou light plane
Lung Chiang class fast attack craft

Source: *World Armaments and Disarmament*, Stockholm International Peace Research Institute [SIPRI] Yearbooks (New York: Oxford University Press, 1970–90).

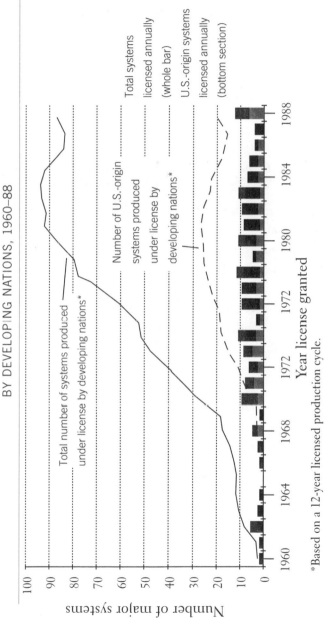

FIGURE 4.4. ESTIMATED LICENSED PRODUCTION OF MAJOR CONVENTIONAL WEAPON SYSTEMS BY DEVELOPING NATIONS, 1960–88

*Based on a 12-year licensed production cycle.

Source: U.S. Congress, Office of Technology Assessment (OTA), *Global Arms Trade: Commerce in Advanced Military Technology and Weapons*, OTA-ISC-460 (Washington, D.C.: U.S. Government Printing Office), p. 9, fig. 1.9.

TABLE 4.5. NUMBER OF MAJOR WEAPON SYSTEMS LICENSED

1961–65	41
1966–70	44
1971–75	68
1976–80	99
1981–85	93
1986–90	86
1991–95 (e)	50

Source: Defense Budget Project, *Database on International Collaboration in Military Production* (Washington, D.C.: Defense Budget Project, 1995).

Licenses database is comprised of major weapon systems that have been licensed from one country to another since 1961. Table 4.5 indicates that international licensing became a brisk business by the 1960s, with eighty-five systems entering licensed production during that decade. In the decade of the 1970s, that number nearly doubled to reach 167, and increased to 179 in the 1980s.

It is no coincidence that an increasing number of newly industrialized and developing nations attained significant military industrial capacity and entered the arms export business during the 1980s. Between 1978 and 1988, the arms exported by Israel, Brazil, Spain, and South Korea amounted to $16 billion. The increasing number of producers, from both advanced industrial and developing nations, has created a buyers' market in which modern military equipment is generally available to anyone who can pay for it.

From these and many more examples of international collaboration in military technology, a coherent picture begins to emerge. International licensed production of major weapons is ordinary. Codevelopment and coproduction of components and weapon systems among armaments firms of different nations is rising steadily. Major arms firms now engage in international mergers, acquisitions, corporate alliances, and subcontracting to gain access to foreign technology and markets. With the reduction of ideological and nationalist orientations, the development, manufacture, and marketing of powerful conventional weapons begins to resemble other sectors in the international economy.

5 POLITICS OF THE GLOBAL
ARMS ENTERPRISE

THE STRUGGLE FOR LTV

In the early 1990s, foreign business figured prominently in the plans of even the largest U.S. arms companies. Industry giant General Dynamics expected foreign business to increase from 17 percent of sales in the mid-1980s to about 50 percent by the mid-1990s, and Martin Marietta forecast that foreign sales would more than double from 8 percent in 1991 to 20 percent in 1994.[1] Increasingly, large-scale military industrial enterprises, loosed from their ideological moorings, sought global markets, strategic business alliances, and international production arrangements—irrespective of national boundaries and loyalties.

In the spring of 1992, for example, the French military conglomerate, Thomson-CSF, and Hughes Aircraft Company bid $280 million for the Missiles Division of the LTV Aerospace and Defense Company.[2] They topped a recent offer by two U.S. arms companies, Martin Marietta and Lockheed. As one of the twenty largest U.S. arms makers, LTV engaged in the development, production, and marketing of many sensitive and highly classified weapons, some requiring top secret and special access clearances. The Missiles Division was a leading supplier of rocket artillery, tactical missiles, and related weapons; it produced the Multiple Launch Rocket System (MLRS), the Army Tactical Missile System (ATACMS), which can be armed with nuclear and chemical warheads, the Extended Range Interceptor (ERINT), an antitactical ballistic missile system, and the Line-of-Sight Antitank (LOSAT) missile, among others. Thomson planned to upgrade LTV's capabilities by infusing French capital and technology.

In 1990, Thomson-AG, the parent company, ranked as the world's second largest military electronics house, with $6.8 billion in revenues. It sold military equipment to about 100 countries. Sixty-one percent of Thomson's revenues were from export sales, including 26 percent to the Middle East and 9 percent to the United States.[3] Thomson had previously acquired some twelve U.S. defense subsidiaries, including Wilcox Electric (1988) and Alsys Corp. (1991), with a combined work force of about fourteen hundred people and annual sales of about $225 million.[4] Thomson's bid for the LTV Missiles Division fit nicely into the company's overall business strategy. "Thomson-CSF's overriding aim is," according to its chairman and president, "to ensure that each of its core business groups . . . has the critical mass to lead and grow in a competitive global marketplace. The company pursues mergers, acquisitions, and strategic alliances in order to strengthen its position in worldwide defense markets."[5] Thomson's move to acquire LTV represented the company's desire to achieve technical acumen, production economies of scale, and a lasting presence in the world's largest arms market. By most measures, the Thomson bid for LTV was an order of magnitude larger than its previous defense acquisitions in the United States.

Thomson was in a position to evaluate the Missile Division because LTV developed the hypersonic VT-1 Missile under contract for Thomson's Crotale NG short-range air defense weapon system that is sold internationally.[6] In September 1991, Thomson announced it would transfer technology and production of the VT-1 Missile from LTV's Texas facilities to Germany and France as part of the Euromissile consortium of Messerschmitt-Bölkow-Blohm GmbH (MBB) and Aerospatiale.[7] Thomson is engaged in joint development and other business activities with arms firms worldwide. In describing Thomson's relationship with McDonnell Douglas, for example, a company spokesman said, "Thomson-CSF has set up strategic alliances around the world. With our expertise in diode-pumped laser technology, this venture will allow Thomson and McDonnell Douglas to pursue complementary objectives involving laser products on a global basis."[8] Thomson's global business strategy is partly subsidized by the French government, which owns 60 percent of the company.

Perhaps the French were encouraged by their experience in Europe where cross-border consortia and joint ventures involving arms companies are ordinary. Examples abound: the Alpha Jet (Dassault and Dornier), Eurocopter (Aerospatiale and MBB), Sepecat (Dassault and British Aerospace), Euromissile (Aerospatiale and MBB), Dragon (Thomson-CSF and Thyssen), Martel (Matra and British Aerospace), Apache (Matra and MBB), Mobidic (Aerospatiale, Thomson-Brandt, Dornier, and Diehl), and Brevel (Matra and MBB), to cite a few examples. Perhaps they were emboldened by the quickening pace of transatlantic acquisitions.

A classic battle played out in the committee rooms on Capitol Hill. Former U.S. Secretary of Defense Frank Carlucci, now vice chairman of the Carlyle Group, which was seeking to acquire the Aircraft Division of LTV, represented Thomson (and the French government) before the Senate and House Armed Services Committees. He argued that Thomson should be permitted to acquire LTV's Missile Division because the French company performed successfully as a Department of Defense contractor for ten years on "a wide variety of critically important programs valued at nearly $1.5 billion . . . includ[ing] more than 20 classified programs, some classified above the secret level." He cited extensive collaboration already existing between Thomson and major U.S. arms firms: GTE (on the MSE battle communication system), Hughes and TRW (on missile defense), Raytheon and Hughes (on sonars), McDonnell Douglas (on high-energy lasers), LTV (on hypersonic missiles), United Technologies (on helicopter displays), and Martin Marietta (on tactical missiles).[9] "[T]he U.S. cannot escape the trend toward greater internationalization of western defense industry," he argued. " 'Fortress America' is not an option."[10]

Norm Augustine, then chairman and CEO of Martin Marietta Corporation, also sought to acquire LTV's Missile Division. He contended that Thomson's bid should be rejected because a majority of Thomson was owned by the French government. "[O]ur policy," he said, "should be simply to prohibit foreign government ownership of defense suppliers like LTV."[11] He distinguished rigorously between public and private acquisition of a foreign firm, approving of the 1989 sale of Fairchild Space & Defense to Matra, the French missile company, for $235 million. Like Carlucci, he cited the trend toward global military industry. From 1988 to 1992, he said, more than sixty U.S. arms makers were sold for more than $10 billion; "[i]ncreasingly, U.S. defense firms, including aerospace firms, have been sold to foreign companies."[12]

In the end, Augustine's view prevailed and Thomson withdrew its bid for LTV, convinced that the Congress and the U.S. Department of Defense would not permit a foreign government to acquire a premier U.S. military industrial asset like LTV. But the principle of acquisition of arms companies in the United States by private foreign firms was never challenged during the debate. Indeed, as Augustine noted, the pace of large-scale acquisition of U.S. arms firms by European firms had quickened over the past several years, including sale of Singer's Electronic Systems Division to Plessey for $500 million (1988), the sale of Honeywell's Federal Systems to Bull HN of France for $100 million (1990), the Aerospatiale/Alcatel/Alenia acquisition of 49 percent of Ford Aerospace's Space Systems for $182 million (1990), and the 1992 acquisition of General Motors's Allison Transmissions by ZF Friedrichshafen AG of Germany.[13]

Even the Committee on Foreign Investment in the United States (CFIUS), which reviewed the Thomson bid from a national security standpoint, demonstrated minimal concern over foreign acquisition of U.S. arms firms. From its inception in August 1988 though May 1992, CFIUS examined over seven hundred investments and prohibited only one. The debate over LTV failed to focus on the critical element, that globalization of military business weakens national and international controls over weapons technology and arms exports. It was, instead, a public face-off between competing suitors of the bankrupt LTV corporation. In the end, the LTV Missiles Division was acquired by Loral for $261 million. Not to be dissuaded, Carlucci and the Carlyle Group found a new partner, the

Northrop Corporation, and acquired the LTV Aircraft Division for $214 million.[14]

The LTV events provided an opportunity and even a precedent to discourage the further integration of different nationally oriented military industries. Following the LTV debacle, newspaper reports forecast a tougher U.S. government stance against foreign takeovers of sensitive military industrial assets like LTV. According to one contemporary account, the Department of Defense was "mulling especially restrictive security requirements for foreign-controlled defense companies operating in the U.S." It predicted that if Bill Clinton became president, the environment for foreign firms hoping to acquire U.S. arms makers would become "even more inhospitable," not just in the military sector, but for high-technology industries generally.[15] Despite these forebodings the only real action was an amendment to the FY 1993 Defense Authorization Act, which would prohibit firms owned by a foreign government from acquiring large-scale U.S. arms firms.[16]

But this action by the U.S. Congress pushed uphill against powerful economic forces of industrial consolidation. By December 1993, Thomson-CSF had recovered sufficiently from the trauma of LTV to set its sights on yet another U.S. arms firm, Rediffusion. And by late 1994, Rolls-Royce judged the political climate to be calm enough to bid $525 million for the Allison Engine Company, a military engine supplier that would give it a manufacturing and marketing presence in the United States. Over the past several years, Allison had undertaken a $1.8-billion engine development program, funded largely by the U.S. government. Rolls hoped to take it over for a fraction of the cost, and to use Allison's other assets to move into new areas of the U.S. aerospace sector.[17]

As is often the case, international industry proved to be far more flexible and fleet than government policy. While the United States and other leading weapons producers in the West struggled to enunciate rational military industrial policies, the arms industries of Europe and America adjusted to a new era of decreased international demand for advanced weapons and rapidly contracting national acquisition budgets. This response started earlier in Europe and took varied forms in different countries, but on both continents, it involved massive layoffs, mergers, acquisitions, rationalization, and aggressive efforts to access foreign markets through international strategic alliances, teaming arrangements, codevelopment, and other forms of cooperation in military technology.

THE PENTAGON INITIATIVES

Far from discouraging foreign investment in U.S. arms companies and other types of multinational defense business, high-level Clinton defense appointees sought to further the integration of global military production and markets. They took the position that massive arms sales following the Persian Gulf War could not be replicated in the mid-1990s, and therefore could not be counted on to sustain production lines in the U.S. At a luncheon address to journalists in Washington, John M. Deutch, then undersecretary of defense for acquisition and technology, addressed the problem, as he put it, of affording to sustain military readiness on level or declining defense budgets.[18] He presented three main options.

First, the level of infrastructure in the Department of Defense would be reduced through base closings, retirement of marginal equipment, and the like. Second, weapons acquisition policies would be reformed to encourage greater integration of civil and military products and technology. In a sharp departure from past policy, he stated that the United States could no longer afford a separate military industrial base. Although some items, such as high-performance aircraft and submarines, could be procured only in the military sector, he estimated that more than 60 percent of all military items could be obtained from civil industry. These reforms, he thought, would make U.S. industry more competitive, and give the Department of Defense access to more advanced civil innovations.

Although Deutch's comments on acquisition reform were radical in Department of Defense terms, there was nothing new about them. In 1989, for example, a study by the Office of Technology Assessment (OTA) identified the problem:

> Two relatively separate economic sectors have evolved in the post-World War II period, one military and the other commercial. Business practices in the two diverge significantly, and substantial barriers impede the transfer of advanced technology between one sector and the other.[19]

Deutch, Defense Secretary William J. Perry, and arms industry analyst Jacques S. Gansler had all participated in the congressional study. With Perry and Deutch holding the number one and two spots at the Department of Defense, they were in a position to implement their long-standing views on acquisition reform. As Gansler saw it, the Clinton administration could enhance both the competitiveness of U.S. industry and national security. "The key," he wrote, "is to foster a greater integration of the Defence industrial base into the commercial economy . . . [by] increasing the U.S. Department of Defense's reliance on commercial business practices, technologies, factories, and products."[20]

This orientation reflected an ongoing process, led by Perry, and known to insiders at the Office of the Secretary of Defense (OSD) as the "Blueprint for Change." For many years Perry had been a relentless critic of the Department of Defense propensity to hive off technology development from the commercial economy. Blue ribbon panels had produced report after report detailing the inefficiency of the military acquisition system. Perry had influenced many of them.[21] His highly sophisticated and refined style of argumentation was ultimately grounded in a recognition of the superior innovative capacities of commercial industry. He and Deutch together confronted the need to achieve efficiencies in military technology development and production to offset exponential increases in the cost of information-intensive military systems. The "Blueprint" was a way to gain consensus and authority within the Department of Defense, to tear down the military specifications and standards that created a Pentagon-based economy housed in a separate military industrial sector.[22]

Finally, Deutch argued that the international marketplace for arms did not represent a viable option for U.S. arms makers to offset losses associated with reduced U.S. government procurement. Overcapacity in the U.S., Europe, and Russia, combined with falling demand at home and in the developing world, would inevitably lead to price competition. U.S. companies would be forced to reduce their prices too far. Sustaining high levels of arms exports, in his view, was clearly insufficient as a long-term strategy for arms makers.

In a buyers' market, major sales become a contest in which U.S., European, and other firms compete to see which is willing to sell the most military technology at the lowest price. Sometimes firms from the same nation may be pitted one against the other, as, for example, in the transfer of advanced U.S. fighter technology to South Korea. In 1989, South Korea agreed to buy 120 twin-engine F/A-18 fighter aircraft from McDonnell Douglas for $5 billion, with twelve planes to be purchased off-the-shelf, thirty-six assembled from U.S.-built kits, and seventy-two produced under license in Korea. But by 1991, the price had risen to $6.2 billion, and the Koreans demanded sophisticated radar, software, and composite materials technologies that the company was reluctant to release. After nearly two years, South Korea broke off negotiations with McDonnell and decided to buy the F-16 fighter from General Dynamics (now Lockheed Martin) instead. The company's ability to offer the F-16 at a lower price and add additional technology, an advanced radar, and air-to-air missiles, were decisive factors.[23]

Beyond the Korean example, Deutch's observation has, in recent years, been confirmed time and again by the intense price competition between Lockheed Fort Worth Co. and McDonnell Douglas Corp. over international sales of the F-16 and F/A-18 fighter aircraft. As table 5.1 shows, Lockheed was clearly winning the competition; McDonnell Douglas was fighting for survival. Both companies slashed prices to offer the lowest price to foreign customers.

Head-to-head price competition for foreign sales also threatened to undermine the Pentagon's Foreign Military Sales (FMS) program, because it hampered the U.S. government's ability to procure new weapons and transfer them to foreign buyers at the low prices offered by competing companies. The alternative policy, which Deutch advocated, was to further the development of the international military industrial base with our allies, building on established linkages between the U.S. arms industry and its counterparts in Europe and Asia.

He outlined a procurement strategy that called for cooperation of companies and defense ministries of different nations at the earliest stages of weapons development. Although this had met with little

TABLE 5.1. PRICE COMPETITION BETWEEN THE LOCKHEED F-16
AND McDONNELL DOUGLAS F/A-18 FIGHTERS

	Done Deals	Winner
Europe		
Belgium	160 F-16s	Lockheed
Denmark	70 F-16s	Lockheed
Netherlands	213 F-16s	Lockheed
Norway	74 F-16s	Lockheed
Portugal	20 F-16s	Lockheed
Turkey	240 F-16s	Lockheed
Greece	80 F-16s	Lockheed
Spain	72 F/A-18s	McDonnell
Switzerland	34 F/A-18s	McDonnell
Finland	64 F/A-18s	McDonnell
Middle East		
Israel	210 F-16s	Lockheed
Egypt	174 F-16s	Lockheed
Bahrain	12 F-16s	Lockheed
Kuwait	40 F/A-18s	McDonnell
Asia		
Pakistan	68 F-16s	Lockheed
South Korea	160 F-16s	Lockheed
Singapore	26 F-16s	Lockheed
Thailand	36 F-16s	Lockheed
Indonesia	12 F-16s	Lockheed
Taiwan	150 F-16s	Lockheed
Australia	75 F/A-18s	McDonnell
Malaysia	8 F/A-18s	McDonnell
The Americas		
Venezuela	24 F-16s	Lockheed
Canada	138 F/A-18s	McDonnell
Lockheed Subtotal	1,729 F-16s	
McDonnell Subtotal	431 F/A-18s	
Total	2,160	

Source: *Defense News*, September 12–18, 1994, p. 1.

success in the past, with increasing integration of civil and military industry around the world, and incentives to achieve mutual market access on both sides of the Atlantic, it might yet prove to be a viable option. At the Farnborough International air show in September 1994, for example, arms industry executives described a trend toward increasing transatlantic strategic alliances among arms firms. As one vice president of McDonnell Douglas Corporation put it, "The successful defense firms will be those that are most creative in aligning with a variety of partners across borders and signing multilateral memorandums of understanding."[24] Although Deutch had painted with broad brushstrokes, glossing over the specifics, it was clear that the new strategy involved three principal elements: close technical and production cooperation at the industrial level, a reform of the defense acquisition regulations to encourage civil participation, and agreements with our allies for joint development of military technology and procurement of future weapon systems.

These ideas would inform the Clinton administration's long-delayed policy on conventional arms transfers, which would culminate in Presidential Directive 41 (PD41) on that subject. In an internal Department of Defense memorandum of late 1993 that fed into PD41, Deutch made it clear that Department of Defense conventional arms export policy should no longer be entrusted to the Defense Security Assistance Agency (DSAA), which runs the U.S. Foreign Military Sales program. In his view, DSAA had given too much priority to exporting finished weapon systems at the expense of international collaboration. Closer attention at the highest levels of the department would be required to coordinate policy on international acquisition, joint technology development with our allies, and export of conventional arms:

The entire point of the initiatives that Bill Perry and I have been trying to promote is to go considerably beyond the historically foreign
military sales of finished items to technology sharing and joint development. My basic point is that we will not fare well in the future international market place unless we are prepared to share technology; this
is our comparative advantage.[25]

Subsequent to this memo, Deutch proposed a "Circle of Friends"
policy to permit the transfer of conventional weapons technology to
a designated group of close U.S. allies who would agree not to dis-
seminate it further. International teaming, codevelopment, and other
forms of transferring of military technology among the United States
within the "circle" would be presumed to be in the interests of all
participating parties, and would therefore be routinely approved. It
constituted a signal to U.S. military industrialists that they should
extend and build on existing international strategic alliances, that
government was increasingly ready to treat the military sector as if it
was just another sector of the global economy.

European Integration

Although these ideas represented a departure from U.S. policies, to
a large extent, they echoed developments over the past decade in
Europe. For many years, the major arms-producing nations—
France, the United Kingdom, Germany, and Italy—had increased
their reliance on cooperative weapons production and on exports to
finance the ever-increasing costs of research and development. In
the late 1980s, for example, exports accounted for between 33 and
42 percent of all French production. For this reason, the potential
for exports is a major consideration both in the decision to launch a

new program and in the timing of production.[26] The export imperative led, in particular, to promiscuous French arms exports, for
example, to Iraq throughout the 1980s, and more recently, in 1994
when France sold three Agosta 90B submarines to Pakistan, shifting
the balance of power in the Indian Ocean.[27] The dramatic decline in
French export sales, due in part to the poor performance of French
weapons in the Persian Gulf War, significantly weakened the military
industrial sector in France, providing strong impetus for international collaboration in all phases of arms production.

As the decade of the 1980s wore on, it became crystal clear that
no single European nation could continue to develop and produce a
full range of advanced technology weapons.[28] To reach minimum
efficient economies of scale, international collaboration in production became commonplace, and the principal of *juste retour* was
employed to allocate work shares for production of the final product,
usually in proportion to the financial commitment made by the participating nations. This formula often led to redundant production
lines, aggravating the problem of overcapacity in the arms industries, and increasing the overall costs for development and production of particular weapon systems. But it also reduced the financial
commitment of the partners, enabling France, Germany, and the
United Kingdom, among others, to sustain a more extensive and
technologically sophisticated military industrial base than would
otherwise have been possible. In this way, *juste retour* retarded the
development of a truly integrated arms production sector in Europe
during the 1970s and 1980s.

The result was an odd mixture of nationally oriented military
industrial policies with export-led arms production strategies at one
level, and extensive international cooperation among the major arms
producers of Europe at another. Although the specific approaches

differed from country to country, France, the United Kingdom, and Germany all took the necessary steps to establish and preserve highly capable national champions in the most important sectors of the arms industry: aerospace, military electronics, land systems, and military shipbuilding. Nevertheless, as the 1980s drew to a close, national governments in Europe conceded that future military systems would have to be developed on a pan-European basis. In the West, only the United States retained the ability to go it alone and to support several companies in each of the principal arms industries, and even that capability had come into question by the mid-1990s. As one authority suggested in 1992:

Collaborative arms development and coordinated procurement among European producers is merely an extension of arms export strategies. The leap from arms transfers that already include technology transfers or production offsets to fully shared production is small: technology, production and R&D costs are simply divided on a more formal and explicit basis (between relative equals), in return for which a larger and more stable market for the final product is guaranteed.[29]

The evolution of pan-European collaboration is particularly clear in the area of missile production. In the 1970s, European firms produced systems such as the Hawk and the Sidewinder under licensed production agreements with firms in the United States. As they gained knowledge and capability, firms such as Matra, MBB, and British Aerospace gradually began to develop and produce their own missile systems. But by the mid-1980s however, as the costs and technological sophistication of new missiles accelerated, European companies increasingly sought international partners. One study conducted by the Swedish Defense Research Establishment summarized the development of the European missile industry as follows: "Having built up their expertise through production of American missiles under license, the European defense industries switched to national projects during the 1970s. From the mid-1980s on, there has been a shift from national to European projects."[30] This view is supported by table 5.2, which shows that the number of European international missiles projects rose from six in 1970 (with fifteen participating firms) to twenty-five in 1990 (with twenty-five participating firms).

In the 1990s, the long-term trend toward consolidation and internationalization of the European arms industries has been deepened by two system-level events: economic and political union pursuant to the Single European Act, and the transformation of European security arrangements at the end of the cold war.[31] In the wake of the 1986 decision to effect European economic integration, the arms makers of Europe, many of whom also conducted much business in

TABLE 5.2. GROWTH IN INTERNATIONAL COLLABORATION
BY WESTERN EUROPEAN COMPANIES IN THE
DEVELOPMENT OF MISSILES, 1970–90

Year	WE firms	U.S. firms	Intn'l Projects
1970	13	2	6
1975	10	3	11
1980	10	4	14
1985	18	5	18
1990	19	6	25

Source: Compiled from Madelene Sandstrom and Christina Wilen, *A Changing European Defense Industry: The Trend Towards Internationalization in the Defense Industry of Western Europe*, pamphlet (Sundyberg, Sweden: Swedish Defense Research Establishment, Department of Defense Analysis, Institution of Defense Economy and Management, 1994), pp. 48–53, figs. 3.2, 3.6.

the civil sector, entered into a period of intense national and cross-border consolidation. From 1988 through 1992 there were more than ninety major international acquisitions, joint ventures, and collaborative programs that involved a European arms maker.[32] Of those, twenty-two projects included firms based in the United States, most of which entailed cooperation via strategic alliances that did not require a joint venture or an exchange of equity.

Although authority over the arms industries is reserved to the individual nations by Article 223 of the 1958 Treaty of Rome, and was nominally preserved at Maastricht in 1992, in recent years Brussels has become progressively more involved in the arms industry and security issues.[33] This has occurred as a natural consequence of the combination of civil and military technologies and capabilities within the same group of companies and even within individual firms. According to a report by the Office of Technology Assessment, French arms industry officials expressed their belief that "relatively few technologies are uniquely military. The commercial market has become the primary driver in a growing number of defense-related areas, including satellites, electronic components, computers, flat-panel displays, and telecommunications."[34] This view is also widely echoed in Europe, where it has become increasingly difficult to extend special treatment to the military sector, both from the perspective of national governments and from that of international business groups where military equipment is an important element—but by no means represents the majority—of their business. As one authority suggests:

> For companies the consequences of the Single Market are obvious. They have to strengthen their competitiveness, through rationalization, co-operation and mergers. . . . Companies with interests in arms production could not make an exception. Their civilian businesses had

to be reshaped anyway, and it makes no corporate sense to keep arms production separate. Although arms production seldom dominated company decision-making, its corporate structures were substantially changed through a large number of mergers, acquisitions and co-operation agreements. The fast pace at which arms production units were shed and bought, merged and split was unusual if compared to past behavior in the arms production sector, although not if compared to what happened in many civilian sectors.[35]

Some observers of military industrial reorganization in Europe downplay its significance. They emphasize the national quality of the arms industries in Western Europe, the fact that competency for them still resides with the member-states of the European Union, and finally that many arms firms in Western Europe are still state-owned.[36] Other analysts discern "signs of a growing disjunction within Europe," a kind of waffling or disabling of European economic and political union, that could retard full structural integration of the Western European arms industries.[37] But even these observers concede that nationally oriented military industrial policies in Europe are probably untenable in the long term.

Leading European military industrialists, such as Henri Martre, chairman of Aerospatiale, have openly called for a European arms procurement agency that would promote further integration of the European armaments sector.[38] France has stepped up its efforts in support of a European Union arms industry with its "Military Program Law for 1995–2000," which one Délégation Générale pour l'Armement (DGA) official asserted "marked an end to the concept of national independence" in the production of weapon systems in Europe.[39] The intent of these measures is to achieve technological synergy and economies of scale to meet intense competition from a far larger and more dynamic U.S. armaments industry. One analyst, relying on a narrow economic perspective, predicted in 1994 that the United States would soon achieve monopoly power in global military business.[40] But this view underestimates the resolve of the Europeans. Even the French, who pride themselves on nationalism when it comes to military matters, have taken active steps to promote more integrated arms production within Western Europe.

At the opening session of the Centre des Hautes Études de l'Armement in late 1994, where French military industrial policy is often enunciated, Defense Minister François Leotard articulated a European position. "There cannot be," he said, "a [European] defense policy if it is not supported by a strong industrial base, [having in Europe] all the expertise needed to develop the weapons of tomorrow." His plan called for further consolidation, an expansion of pan-European collaboration, and ultimate integration of the arms industries of Western Europe. As the European nation with the most independent arms industry, he asserted, "France has a special role to play in this common strategy, whose only goal is to [perpetuate] the European industrial base."[41] That goal includes the creation of both bilateral and multilateral instruments for the integration of the European arms industries such as the Western European Armaments Group, an enhanced role for the Western European Union under the terms of the Maastricht Treaty, and the expansion of the Franco-German armaments agency in November to include Belgium, Italy, the Netherlands, and probably the United Kingdom.[42]

In the final analysis, the breakup of the Soviet Union and the removal of Russian forces from Europe weakened the political will of the Western European states to maintain redundant capabilities in the arms industries from one nation to another. Such an enterprise would be fundamentally discordant with the thoroughgoing economic integration that is now a fait accompli. In the absence of a palpable threat, it is unlikely the voters of Europe can be convinced to tolerate large-scale budget allocations required to support nationally oriented arms industries, particularly in an era when more military spending involves a highly visible and direct trade-off for social services. Under these circumstances, few if any states are likely to continue to invest in a full-scale national arms industry when a European alternative is available.

In Europe as in the United States, structural adjustment of the arms sector to an industry-wide economic downturn has far outpaced the ability of governments to implement guiding policies; but it was equally clear that governments did not impede industry-led restructuring. Despite the discordant views, the economic and political logic of a common arms industry is likely to prevail. As the research department of one European defense ministry has suggested:

> The debate currently taking place in journals and the literature about the advantages and disadvantages of defense industry cooperation is no longer entirely relevant. While politicians, defense executives and researchers discuss whether international acquisitions and cooperation are good or bad, the companies are acting. Whether the objectives of the governments or the companies will eventually be fulfilled is not clear. What is clear is that the force of initiative and the strength [of] relationships in materiel production have undergone a change.[43]

If industry seemed to take the lead in Europe at the end of the cold war, the ultimate structure of the European arms sector and its relationship to U.S. industry is still evolving. In one scenario, consolidation would lead to a Fortress Europe arms industry, highly subsidized and isolated from its U.S. counterpart through restrictions on trade and direct investment. In another, civil-military integration in Europe and in America would increase global production and sourcing of dual-use technology and components for U.S.- and European-made weapon systems. In a third version, direct integration of the U.S. and European military industrial bases could be facilitated by government, partly through diplomatic initiative and partly through relaxation of U.S. regulations that govern military procurement, and of U.S. export controls, for both military and dual-use technologies. Options two and three were closest to the intent of the Clinton appointees.

A Circle of Friends

In the mid-1990s, top Pentagon officials hoped to offset falling military budgets, and the rising cost of developing weapons, by engaging the forces of global economic and technological integration. They sought to achieve both economies of scale and synergies in technology development within a circle of trusted allies. But to do so required a shift in the logic of U.S. arms transfer policy. The policy of the Bush administration did not depend on the logic of the cold war, which had justified the transfer of military hardware and technology to U.S. friends and allies on the basis of maintaining a balance of power, not only in Europe, but also among U.S. and USSR surrogates in the developing world. The Bush policy, as discussed in chapter 3, treated arms transfers as instruments of foreign policy, instruments that could be selectively applied to accommodate geostrategic circumstances prevailing in the region to which the weapons or military technology were destined. It was driven by calculations of military balance, political cachet, and economic return. Both the cold war and subsequent Bush policies encouraged the transfer of technology to U.S. allies, usually through licensed production of whole weapon systems, as in the transfer of F-16 fighter technology, for example, to South Korea for indigenous production of the Korean fighter plane or the transfer of Trident submarine technology to Britain. But after the mid-1980s, U.S. policy also envisioned codevelopment of weapon systems with close allies, often, but not always on a government-to-government basis. During the Bush administration, two principal instances involving collaboration in the *development* of military technology were the Nunn codevelopment programs within NATO and the FS-X advanced fighter with Japan. A brief discussion of the Nunn programs is warranted here, because although they failed to achieve what their promoters intended, they set a benchmark against which to gage the policies of the Clinton administration, launched in early 1993 as the Perry Initiatives. The FS-X codevelopment of a next-generation Japanese fighter is discussed in chapter 4.

Starting with the fiscal year 1986 Defense Authorization Act, and over the next four years, Congress authorized $666 million to fund cooperative R&D for weapon systems within the NATO Alliance. Each weapons program required a formal government-to-government agreement before funds could be committed. The initial group of Nunn programs began with seven candidates, agreed to in February 1986 at NATO headquarters in Brussels. By 1989, the list had grown to twenty-eight programs under contract, with nineteen in various stages of negotiation.[44] Although they constituted the principal means for the U.S. Defense Department to engage in joint development of weapons with the European allies, the Nunn amendment programs were plagued with difficulties from the start. Several key programs

167

were abandoned early on, including the NATO Frigate Replacement (NFR90), the NATO Anti-Air Warfare System (NAAWS), the Autonomous Precision Guided Munitions (APGM), and the Modular Stand-Off Weapon (MSOW). In others, such as the NATO Identification System (NIS) and the Multi-Functional Information Distribution System (MIDS), one or more of the allies pulled out.

While each failed attempt is a separate story, there were common features, most of them resulting from the fact that the collaboration was conducted formally among several governments. In the NATO Frigate, for example, the participating governments could not agree on a single set of military requirements to satisfy diverse geographical and strategic concerns. The Nunn programs were also hindered by the multiplication of government regulations and bureaucratic requirements of different nations. There was little incentive to work together, and many reasons not to. In addition, on the U.S. side, the military services initially viewed the Nunn funding as an extra pot of money to be applied to projects of low priority to U.S. war-fighting capabilities. Overall, the Nunn programs demonstrated that transatlantic government-to-government collaboration is a difficult, if not impossible undertaking: few met with success and funding for the programs was terminated.

The failure of the Nunn programs, however, did not indicate that technology transfer from the United States to Europe was an unworkable proposition. Indeed, numerous systems developed in the United States, such as the F-16, the NATO AWACS, the Stinger Missile, and the Patriot air defense system, had been successfully replicated in Europe under license, through coproduction agreements and the like. Following the Second World War, the Europeans had used U.S. technology to rebuild their arms industries. The Nunn programs were symptomatic of the problems governments face in managing international cooperation in the development of complex weapon systems. Beyond the difficulty of harmonizing military requirements and added regulatory complexity, leaders of different nations are accountable to different domestic constituencies, such as labor, local arms firms, and local politicians who are often reluctant to share government procurement funds, employment, or the benefits of high-technology explorations with foreign firms.

Industry-to-industry collaboration, however, has long been the preferred means and primary conduit for international cooperation. It can and does take almost as many forms as there are entrepreneurs willing to participate, as is shown in table 4.2 in chapter 4. In recent years, there has been a shift up the ladder of collaboration toward more codevelopment and other forms of complex technical cooperation. The major incentive is economic: industry seeks access to foreign markets. Deals are structured so that participating firms can lever their technologies and maximize profits, irrespective of national origins, loyalties, and political constituencies. Industry-to-industry cooperation, in the absence of government mediation, enables companies to suboptimize for individual gain, where national interest and concerns of governments may or may not be factored into the economic equation. All this is, of course, natural and necessary in the conduct of multinational business in the civil sector.

International military business is different. Few arms companies are private sector entities in the way that commercial industry is. In France, for example, fully three-quarters of the arms makers are owned by the state. But beyond that, the development of most weapon systems, particularly in the United States, is conducted using public funds. Companies are even reimbursed for so-called "independent" R&D not conducted under contract with the government, and for their costs in preparing bids and proposals to compete for government business. They are creatures of the state, funded by the public, whose products are bought and controlled by governments. But their behavior increasingly mirrors the conduct of multinational corporations engaged in other sectors of the global economy.

Two lessons emerged from the Nunn programs. One was learned and the other was not. The first is that because governments are captured by parochial interests, they are often unable to collaborate successfully in the *development* of new military technology and weapon systems. They tend to squabble over military requirements and work shares, and to impose regulations that favor locally based companies and labor. If left to their own devices, however, the arms industries of different nations can and do cooperate effectively, but not necessarily in the national interest. They tend to act like multinational corporations, which are less concerned with advancing national goals than with pursuing objectives internal to the firm, principally growth, profits, proprietary technology, strategic alliances, return on investment, and market power.[45] In the nonmilitary commercial sectors of the world economy, the dominant paradigm suggests that national and international economic interests are largely compatible. Far from being a zero sum game, in the postwar period an expanding international economy in virtually every sector has lifted the standard of living among the developed nations of the West. But this understanding is not applicable to the military sectors, where national security and economic growth can be undermined by international commerce in advanced weapons and military technology.

The unlearned lesson was that the military industrial aspects of national security are too important to be decided by international economic forces. The central implication of the emergence of a global arms industry is loss of national controls over military technology. This process might inevitably have been set in train by the gradual ascendance of civil over military technology in the information and electronics industries. Or it might have evolved as a function of the integration of civil and military technology bases in Europe and Asia. But in the United States, it could be hastened or retarded as a matter of public policy. The cold war policy was to transfer military technology en masse to the NATO allies and to other nations with which the U.S. had close security ties. The new policy of the Clinton defense team was to break down the distinction between military and commercial technology at home, and to link up the military industrial bases of the West.

A major component of that strategy was to convince Japanese government officials and corporate leaders to transfer militarily useful technology to their friends in the United States. The history of U.S.-Japan military technology cooperation had, of course, been lopsided with most or all of the technology flowing to Japan. By the end of the 1970s, Pentagon officials began to recognize Japanese technological prowess, and to consider ways to import Japanese commercial technology into U.S. weapon systems. Bill Perry, then President Jimmy Carter's undersecretary of defense for research and engineering, was an early advocate for greater reciprocity in U.S.-Japanese technology exchange. Indeed, he is credited as the motivating force behind the Systems and Technology Forum, a group established in 1980 to promote increased cooperation between the U.S. and Japan in the development of military technology.[46]

But even after a decade of regular consultations on technology issues, the Systems and Technology Forum had failed to produce a two-way street for technology transfer. Indeed, by the mid-1990s, it could accurately be characterized as a technology superhighway to Japan with a dirt path back. When Bill Perry returned to the Pentagon as deputy secretary in 1993, he was determined to rectify this situation, and together with John Deutch, launched the Perry Initiative, "to seek a better balance in the flow of defense technology between the U.S. and Japan."

But this time there was a new twist: the U.S. now sought to trade military technology for Japanese commercial technologies, such as optoelectronics, composite materials, and manufacturing processes, that could be applied to U.S. weapon systems. In what was billed as the "Technology-for-Technology Initiative," Department of Defense officials adopted a tougher stance. Japan would always be permitted to purchase U.S. weapons off-the-shelf, but "significant transfers of U.S. military technology . . . [would] require that Japan provide commercial, military, or dual use technology in return." The Perry-Deutch "approach to defense cooperation with Japan," they argued, "will make the most effective use of the industrial capabilities of both countries."[47]

Like most Americans, U.S. defense officials were naive about Japanese attitudes toward technology absorption and transfer. In Japan, technology acquisition and development is a matter of national security. Japanese government officials and business leaders elevate technology monitoring, identification, acquisition, and absorption to a level of strategic importance exceeding that of most other countries.[48] In their understanding, security rests on both nationally based technological infrastructure and on the ability to tap into foreign-based innovation systems. As John Deutch learned in September 1993—when he presented the Technology-for-Technology proposal to Japanese officials in Tokyo—it is unlikely that Japan would trade commercial technology for U.S. military technology on a "significant" scale because Japanese advanced process technology is far more valuable to Japan than anything the Pentagon might offer.

In this, as in so many other aspects of national security and economic competition, Japan is the exception that proves the rule. Japan simply wanted to continue to acquire U.S. military technology on easy terms as it had for the past several decades. European companies proved far more willing to share both military and commercial technology across national borders. But perhaps more important to this analysis, the global production of sophisticated weapons in the postwar period emanated first from the United States to Europe and Japan, and then from the United States and Europe to the developing world. Japan alone among the advanced industrial states pursued a policy of not exporting military systems and technology. But even that policy began to break down in the 1990s as the distinction between military and commercial technology lost its currency and increasingly advanced commercial technologies found their way into high-technology weapons.

JAPANESE EXCEPTIONALISM

Japan depends on the United States to provide technology for its military aircraft and other weapons platforms. The Mutual Defense Assistance Agreement of 1954 established the legal basis for transfer of U.S. weapons and military technology to Japan. In 1960, the Mutual Cooperation and Security Treaty provided the broad framework for U.S.-Japan security relations for a generation. Of the thirty-six types of aircraft flown by the Japanese Self Defense Forces, nine were purchased directly from the United States, sixteen were coproduced, and several are copies of low-technology U.S. aircraft.[49] Although military production in Japan has remained insignificant in comparison to the commercial sector, table 5.3 shows that the number of major U.S. weapon systems transferred to Japan has been substantial.

In three respects, Japan is a special case. First, the U.S. transfers the production technology for more major weapon systems to Japan than it does to any other nation. In the 1980s, Japan embarked on a rapid arms industry buildup and developed extensive military industrial capabilities, drawing heavily on licensed production from the United States. In the 1990s, the Japanese defense budget continued to expand through 1994, in marked contrast to the military expenditures of the advanced industrial economies of North America and Europe.

Second, concerns that Japan might proliferate U.S.-licensed,

TABLE 5.3. SELECTED U.S. WEAPON SYSTEMS
PRODUCED UNDER LICENSE BY JAPAN

F-15J Eagle fighter aircraft
FS-X fighter aircraft
CH-47 Chinook helicopter
KV-107/2A helicopter
Model 205 UH-1H helicopter
Model 209 AH-1S helicopter
UH-60J helicopter
EP-3C Orion electronic intelligence aircraft
M-110A2 203mm self-propelled howitzer
Patriot missile battery
MIM-104 Patriot mobile surface-to-air missile
MIM-23 Hawk mobile surface-to-air missile
AIM-7F Sparrow air-to-air missile
AIM-9L Sidewinder air-to-air missile
BGM-71C I-TOW anti-tank missile

Source: U.S. Congress, Office of Technology Assessment (OTA), from data in *World Armaments and Disarmament,* Stockholm International Peace Research Institute (SIPRI) Yearbooks (New York: Oxford University Press, 1970–90).

codeveloped, or derivative military technologies are somewhat mitigated by Japan's policy against export of military equipment. Although this policy may change, it is anchored in the larger U.S.-Japan security relationship, and to the extent that this alliance remains stable, Japanese restraint in arms exports will probably be preserved. If, however, trade relations between the two economic superpowers continue to deteriorate, a new security environment could emerge in which Japan depended less on the U.S. security umbrella. Change could also result from different perceptions by the two countries of their roles and interests in the evolving post–cold war security structure. Japan might decide to do what many U.S. policy makers have urged for decades: take on even more of the burden of its own defense and assume a stronger role in international affairs, especially in the Asia-Pacific region. In that case, the United States (and the world) would find a Japan with a strong base of military technology, and an industrial sector fully capable of expanding production swiftly in the event that it was called on to do so.

Third, the flow in military technology between the United States and Japan has been, as suggested above, a one-way street to Japan, with few exceptions. To date, very little Japanese-origin military technology has been transferred to the United States. However, a significant but unknown quantity of Japanese high-technology products (with both civil and military applications) has been incorporated into U.S. weapons, particularly at the lower tiers of the U.S. defense subcontracting base. For example, Japan supplied about $158 million in parts and components for three U.S. Navy weapons programs: the HARM missile, the VERDIN communication system, and the MK-48 torpedo. Of that amount, approximately $81 million was for ceramic packaging for semiconductors, which is not produced competitively in the United States.[50] Overall, government and corporate leaders in Japan appear eager to receive U.S. military technology, and at the same time, reluctant to share theirs with the United States.

If maintained, the U.S. policy to permit frequent transfers of military technology to Japan will continue to build up the military industrial base of that nation, regardless of the success or failure of efforts by Department of Defense to secure dual-use and commercial technology in exchange as contemplated by the Technology-for-Technology initiative. This, of course, raises the question of the rearming of Japan. Japan increased its defense expenditures in real terms by about 6 percent per year throughout the 1980s, and is by for the largest military presence in the Western Pacific. Few believe Japan intends to build its arsenals to levels associated with the Second World War. Nevertheless, a key component of Japanese military industrial strategy is to produce a broad range of major weapons at very low production rates, developing the technological know-how and industrial infrastructure that would have to precede a decision to rearm.

Japan is able to reap the benefits of much U.S. military R&D, essentially buying it through licensed production, returning little or nothing to the U.S. technology base. Japanese officials believe that technology is a precious commodity, and unlike many U.S. arms industry executives, they see it as far more valuable than short-term economic gains. Nevertheless, those who advocate collaboration argue that by transferring military technology to Japan, the United States enhances that nation's ability to assume a greater share of its own defense and that U.S. arms companies are more profitable as a result. These short-term benefits will have to be balanced against the possibility that Japan could change its arms export policies, and that if it does, as many U.S. military contractors believe it will, the

United States will have helped to create yet another participant in the international arms market.

The new initiatives of the Clinton defense appointees replaced the rationale of military balance with the cool technocratic language of economy and efficiency. In an era of plunging military budgets, they recognized better than their predecessors the limitations of an arms transfer policy that sought to bolster domestic military industrial interests through exports of advanced technology weapons to regional hotspots. They hoped to replace it with a policy to promote international development of weapons and the exchange and integration of military and commercial technology, both at home and abroad. The Perry initiatives on one hand, and the consolidation of the European arms industries on the other, added momentum and force to the diffusion of military production that had long been in train.

6 CONCLUSION

This book begins with one paradox, the paradox of international security, and ends with another, the paradox of proliferation: the global spread of knowledge and industrial capability embodies both the promise of development and the threat of annihilation. Nuclear, pharmaceutical, chemical, biological, aerospace, information, materials, and other technologies that lead to wealth and a higher standard of living are also fundamentally implicated in the drive to acquire the most pernicious weapons. Because there cannot be an end of technology, the paradox of proliferation is here to stay.

Two decades ago, U.S. presidential candidate Jimmy Carter took a resolute stand against the weapons trade, making it a major plank in his foreign policy. He announced it on the campaign trail, presented it in a major speech in New York City, and reiterated it in a nationwide radio broadcast following his inauguration. The result of President Carter's strongly held personal conviction was Presidential Directive 13 (PD13), which was issued on May 19, 1977. PD13 viewed "arms transfers as an exceptional foreign policy implement, to be used only in instances where it can be clearly demonstrated that the transfer contributes to our national security interests." It limited the "dollar volume . . . of new commitments under the Foreign Military Sales" program, and stated that the United States would not be the first to transfer advanced weapons into a region "which would create a new or significantly higher combat capability." And perhaps most important, it prohibited the export of U.S. military technology through coproduction agreements.[1]

But the Carter policy was too radical for its time, and it could not be implemented. Few of the president's senior advisers fully supported it. Some saw it as naive or unrealistic in the context of cold war assumptions about Soviet motivations and actions in arming the developing world. They viewed the arms trade as an element of foreign policy, not as an arms control issue. Others feared the administration would be duped by the Europeans, who would seize on unilateral American restraint as an opportunity to increase and consolidate their position in foreign arms markets.[2] Some pandered to the defense lobbyists in Washington who, in time, came to refer to PD13 as "the leprosy letter."

Carter's determination to restrain the arms trade also led to the Conventional Arms Talks with the Soviet Union beginning in December 1977. But after considerable progress, and apparent Soviet acquiescence to American terms, the talks collapsed in the fourth session in Mexico City. The U.S. delegation walked out, refusing to discuss limitations on arms transfers to the "Soviet-proposed regions" of West Asia and East Asia.[3] The next time the issue of restraint in arms trade registered on the political radar scope, it was imbedded in a policy of complete duplicity. In May 1991, the Bush administration proposed talks on arms transfers and nonproliferation among five major arms-exporting nations: the United States, the Soviet Union, the United Kingdom, France, and China. But the U.S. policy of talking arms restraint and simultaneously negotiating record levels of arms exports to the Middle East undermined the five-power talks from the beginning, as is discussed in chapter 3.

Writing in the wake of the failed Carter policy, Andrew Pierre outlined a system of restraints for the international arms trade, which he hoped would be politically palatable. He envisioned ongoing "informal negotiations" among the major Western powers to "regulate" the trade in conventional arms, and provided examples of both qualitative and quantitative restraints. Multilateral coordination of arms transfers, he suggested, "should become a central element of a more common Western approach toward such unstable regions as the Persian Gulf and Middle East." Only after achieving a degree of solidarity with the Europeans would it make sense to approach the Soviet Union over the issue of arms restraint. "The present pattern of competitive, uncoordinated sales," he wrote in 1982, "is contrary to Western political interests."[4]

But Pierre's ideas were never tried. Arms sales today are, if anything, even more competitive and less coordinated than they were a decade ago. The question is whether changed circumstances after the cold war work against or in favor of restraint in the political economy of the global arms trade. There is no question that the breakup of the Soviet Union presented an opportunity to stem the arms trade and slow the globalization of military industry and technology. Probably the best hope of addressing the arms transfer aspect of proliferation would have been to revisit the Carter policy, but with a strong dose of U.S. restraint and multilateral arm-twisting to draw in the other major arms-exporting states. But as chapter 5 has recounted, both the Americans and the Europeans have so far failed to comprehend the challenge, much less rise to it.

With the end of the cold war, the incentive for a mutual foreign policy among the United States and the European powers is greatly reduced, if only because there is no obvious danger to the security of the West. Moreover, the domestic economic aspects of the arms trade have become much more important. The imperative to export arms, to achieve scale economies and access to foreign markets, has only been heightened by reduced military spending after the cold war. Arms exports are not sanctioned on the basis of alliance relations or security policy alone, but increasingly in terms of electoral politics, export revenues, jobs, and the need to achieve greater efficiency in the development of military equipment. It was, in fact, necessary to write a political economy of the arms trade even to pose the paradox of proliferation.

The conditions upon which the paradox rests are both structural and political in character. International collaboration in military technology takes many forms, as demonstrated in chapter 4. Multinational business techniques and organization are becoming more common in the development and production of weapons. The spread of military industry and technology throughout Europe and Asia and into the developing world is increasingly embedded as infrastructure in a global military industrial enterprise. In the post–cold war era, these processes are pushed forward by the application of market forces to military production. Governments appear more willing to accommodate the globalization of military industry, at a historical juncture when it has finally become possible to integrate commercial technology into many aspects of military production.

At the same time, the developing nations aggressively assert their right to a technologically enhanced future. They are less and less willing to tolerate a double standard in which the more advanced industrial states dominate the terms of trade, investment, finance, and the exchange of technology. This extends even to weapons of mass destruction, as negotiations over the renewal of the Nuclear Nonproliferation Treaty have shown. At the end of the twentieth century, the politics of development militate against effective implementation of global nonproliferation norms and regimes.

This book has identified sporadic militarism and proliferation, broadly defined, as threats to the international community and to the stability of the emerging multipolar system of nation-states. But it offers little hope that the West will turn to face this common enemy with common sense. The paradox of proliferation is not easily encapsulated in political slogans, nor is it the stuff of which utopian or idealistic schemes of disarmament are made. It is a tough reality in which history provides both spectacle and farce: for now, the former U.S. and Soviet surrogates in the developing world have been transformed by the end of the cold war into coveted customers.

At its most fundamental level, the task of public policy is to control proliferation of powerful modern weapons of all kinds. But it is a task to which public policy is not particularly well suited, as the history of the arms trade and of proliferation of weapons of mass destruction suggests. It is also a task that political leaders have not taken seriously enough. Most are ready to condemn the further spread of nuclear, biological, and chemical weapons, although some reserve the right to maintain existing arsenals or to build new ones. At the same time, most policy makers condone a vigorous trade in powerful conventional arms, without appreciating their destructive capability or their intimate connection to weapons of mass destruction.

In the end, we are left with only one conclusion: proliferation must be harnessed, but we do not yet have adequate multilateral institutions or the insights required to do it. Yet the consequences of proliferation strike both at the fabric of international relations, as the specter of nuclear weapons in North Korea and Iran attest, and at basic social relations, as shown by the 1995 nerve gas attacks in the Tokyo subway and the bombing of the U.S. government building in Oklahoma City. At one end of the spectrum, rogue states and regional adversaries can weaken the prospects for global peace and stability. At the other, indiscriminate terror can undermine an open society, ushering in an era of personal surveillance as governments act to protect the internal security.[5]

In short, we cannot live with the paradox of proliferation and we cannot live without it. We can isolate its elements and analyze them, but we have not yet developed a political and social understanding sufficient to resolve it. Until we do, we will be like so many idiot savants, chasing the consequences of a global technological enterprise at once more powerful, more beautiful, and more noxious than its creators can comprehend.

NOTES

CHAPTER 1: APPROACH TO ARMAGEDDON

1. Lt. Col. Jeffrey McCausland, "The Gulf Conflict: A Military Analysis," *Adelphi Papers* 282 (November 1993): 21.
2. Figures are calculated from data presented in chap. 3, table 3.5.
3. U.S. Department of Defense, *Conduct of the Persian Gulf War,* Final Report to Congress, Pursuant to Title V of the Persian Gulf Conflict Supplemental Authorization and Personnel Benefits Act of 1991 (P.L. 102-25), April 1992, pp. 15–18.
4. W. Seth Carus and Joseph S. Bermudez, Jr., "Iraq's Al-Husayn Missile Programs," *Jane's Soviet Intelligence Review* (May 1990): 204.

5. Committee for National Security, "The Lessons of Iraq: Unconventional Weapons, Inspection and Verification, and the United Nations and Disarmament," a briefing and discussion with Johan Molander, special adviser to the chairman, United Nations Special Commission on Iraq, November 13, 1991, p. 4.

6. U.S. Department of Defense, *Conduct of the Persian Gulf War*, p. 221.

7. See "Iraq's Suppliers of Unconventional Weapons Technology," prepared by Middle East Defense News (Mednews), March 2, 1991; and Kenneth R. Timmerman, "The Poison Gas Connection: Western Suppliers of Unconventional Weapons and Technologies to Iraq and Libya," a special report commissioned by the Simon Weisenthal Center from Middle East Defense News (Mednews), 1990.

8. U.S. Congress, Office of Technology Assessment (OTA), *Global Arms Trade: Commerce in Advanced Military Technology and Weapons*, OTA-ISC-460 (Washington, D.C.: U.S. Government Printing Office, June 1991), p. 69.

9. In fact, the ninth United Nations/International Atomic Energy Agency inspection of Iraq was conducted in response to information from the German government acknowledging that German firms supplied components for the Iraqi nuclear weapons program. David W. Dorn, "Nuclear Inspections in Iraq: A Case Study," in G. Neuneck and O. Ishebeck, eds., *Missile Proliferation, Missile Defense, and Arms Control*, proceedings of a symposium held at the University of Hamburg, Germany (Baden-Baden: Nomos Verlagsgeselischaft, 1993), pp. 79–90.

10. U.S. Defense Security Assistance Agency officials, interview with author, names and date withheld.

11. Israeli intelligence officials, interview with author, names and date withheld.

12. See U.S. Congress, House Committee on Government Operations, Subcommittee on Commerce, Consumer, and Monetary Affairs, *U.S. Government Controls on Sales to Iraq: Hearing Before the Subcommittee on Commerce, Consumer, and Monetary Affairs*, 101st Cong., 2d sess., September 27, 1990; and Gary Milhollin, *Licensing*

Mass Destruction: U.S. Exports to Iraq: 1985–1990 (Washington, D.C.: Wisconsin Project on Nuclear Arms Control, June 1991), p. 1, passim.

13. Intelligence officials at the Los Alamos Laboratory, interview with author, names and date withheld.

14. The HMS *Sheffield* failed to recognize the incoming Exocet missile as hostile because its antiship missile defenses were programmed to recognize French-made missiles as friendly.

15. ACDA, *World Military Expenditures, 1990*, p. 109.

16. Al Faw and Qasr-e-Sherin/Kermanshah are the sites of the first and last of five great battles in the spring and summer of 1988 in which Iraq smashed Iran's military machine, ending the Iran-Iraq War. See Stephen C. Pelletiere et al., *Iraqi Power and U.S. Security in the Middle East* (Carlisle Barracks, Penn.: U.S. Army War College, Strategic Studies Institute, 1990), p. 25.

17. As the French minister of defense quipped in answer to public outrage over French soldiers facing superior French arms in Iraq, "If you want to be able to afford to make your own weapons, you have to be able to sell them." *Washington Post*, April 6, 1991, p. A17.

18. French DGA (Délégation Générale pour l'Armement) officials, interview with author, names and date withheld.

19. U.S. Department of Defense, Defense Security Assistance Agency (DSAA), *Foreign Military Sales, Foreign Military Construction Sales and Military Assistance Facts* (Washington, D.C.: U.S. Government Printing Office, Sept. 30, 1989), p. 3; and U.S. Department of Defense, DSAA, *Fiscal Year Series* (Washington, D.C.: U.S. Government Printing Office, Sept. 30, 1989), p. 101.

20. French DGA officials, interview. See also Bruce W. Jentleson, *With Friends Like These: Reagan, Bush, and Saddam, 1982–1990* (New York: Norton, 1994), pp. 44–47, and passim for an intriguing analysis of U.S. policy toward Iraq leading up to the Persian Gulf War.

21. White House, Office of the Press Secretary, "Conventional Arms Transfer Policy," Fact Sheet, February 17, 1995, p. 1.

22. White House, Office of the Press Secretary, "Criteria for Decision-making on U.S. Arms Exports," Fact Sheet, February 17, 1995, p. 1.

23. U.S. Department of Defense, Office of the Undersecretary of Defense (Acquisition and Technology), *World-Wide Conventional Arms Trade (1994–2000): A Forecast and Analysis* (Washington, D.C.: Department of Defense, December 1994), pp. v, 28.

24. Testimony by Director of Central Intelligence James Woolsey before the United States Senate Government Affairs Committee, February 24, 1993. Woolsey continued, "As international awareness of the problem increases, countries are becoming more clever in devising networks of front companies and suppliers to frustrate export controls and buy what would otherwise be prohibited to them."

25. Russian Foreign Intelligence, "A New Challenge After the Cold War: The Proliferation of Weapons of Mass Destruction," Report, translated by Foreign Broadcast Information Service, February 1993, p. 1.

26. See Article 51 of the UN Charter.

27. The successor states to the Soviet Union whose territory was subject to CFE limitations—Armenia, Azerbaijan, Belarus, Georgia, Kazakhstan, Moldova, Russia, and Ukraine—agreed to accept the basic principles of the CFE in the Tashkent Agreement of May 15, 1992. "At the Oslo Extraordinary Conference of all 29 CFE participants in June 1992, these eight states confirmed their acceptance of all rights and obligations of the former Soviet Union." U.S. Arms Control and Disarmament Agency (ACDA), "Adherence to and Compliance with Arms Control Agreements and the President's Report to Congress on Soviet Noncompliance with Arms Control Agreements," report, January 14, 1993, p. 15.

28. As table 2.3 in chapter 2 indicates, developing countries of proliferation concern ordered about 1,550 combat aircraft from 1987 through 1992. Some analysts believe that this trade is slowing, and have forecast that "for the rest of the 1990s, international transfers [of combat aircraft] will average between 195 and 280 planes per year." Jonathan Cohen and Andrew Peach, "The Spread of Advanced Combat Aircraft," in Randall Forsberg, ed., *The Arms Production Dilemma* (Cambridge, Mass.: MIT Press, 1994), p. 239.

29. Ian Anthony, ed., *Arms Export Regulations* (Oxford: Oxford University Press and Stockholm International Peace Research Institute [SIPRI], 1991), p. 220.

30. U.S. Congress, Office of Technology Assessment (OTA), *Technologies Underlying Weapons of Mass Destruction*, OTA-BP-ISC-115 (Washington, D.C.: U.S. Government Printing Office, December 1993), p. 244.

31. Janne E. Nolan, *Trappings of Power: Ballistic Missiles in the Third World* (Washington, D.C.: Brookings Institution, 1991), p. 116.

32. U.S. Department of State, Office of the Assistant Secretary/Spokesman, "Statement by Richard Boucher, Spokesman," and attached "Revisions to MTCR Guidelines," January 7, 1993, pp. 1–2.

33. Nolan, *Trappings of Power*, pp. 115–22.

CHAPTER 2: PROLIFERATION

1. United Nations press release, "Special Commission Conducts Exploratory Inspection at Muthanna State Establishment, Iraq's Chemical-Weapon Facility, 9–14 June," IK/27, June 24, 1991, p. 2.

2. United Nations press release, "Sixth Chemical Weapons Inspection in Iraq Carried Out by UN Team," IK/70, November 15, 1991, p. 1.

3. Although eleven sites had been inspected, there was "no evidence of actual weaponization." United Nations press release, "Special Commission Discusses Progress Achieved in Past Six Months to Disarm Iraq, at Plenary Session Held 21–23 October," IAEA/1195, IK/68, October 24, 1991; and United Nations Security Council, "Report by the Executive Chairman of the Special Commission Established by the Secretary-General Pursuant to Paragraph 9(b)(i) of Security Council Resolution 687 (1991)," Annex, S/23165, October 25, 1991, pp. 4–6.

4. United Nations Security Council, "First Report on the Sixth IAEA On-Site Inspection in Iraq Under Security Council Resolution 687

(1991), 22–30 September 1991," Enclosure, S/23122, October 8, 1991, pp. 3–6.

5. "Michel Saint Mleux, expert from France, said the Commission had recently discovered that within one year, Iraq could have had both the fissile material and the weaponization device needed to produce a nuclear explosive device, but at the research and development stage, not at the production stage." United Nations, "Press Briefing by Executive Chairman [Rolf Ekeus] of Special Commission on Disarmament of Iraq," October 24, 1991, p. 1.

6. Bruce W. Jentleson, *With Friends Like These: Reagan, Bush and Saddam, 1982–1990* (New York: Norton, 1994), pp. 105–23, 221–26.

7. Rolf Ekeus, interviewed by George Leopold, "One on One: Rolf Ekeus, Executive Chairman, U.N. Special Commission on Iraq," *Defense News.*

8. "Biological and toxin weapons potentially pose greater dangers than either chemical or nuclear weapons because BTW agents are so lethal on a pound-for-pound bases, their production requires a much smaller and cheaper industrial infrastructure, and the necessary technology and know-how are almost entirely dual-use and thus widely available." U.S. Congress, Office of Technology Assessment (OTA), *Technologies Underlying Weapons of Mass Destruction*, OTA-BP-ISC-115 (Washington, D.C.: U.S. Government Printing Office, December 1993), p. 73.

9. "An apparently diluted form of a nerve gas called sarin . . . was placed simultaneously in five subway cars at morning rush hour, killing 10 victims and sickening thousands more." *Time*, April 3, 1995, p. 28.

10. During the Second World War, Allied firebomb attacks are estimated to have killed up to 100,000 persons in Tokyo and 200,000 in Dresden. U.S. Congress, Office of Technology Assessment (OTA), *Proliferation of Weapons of Mass Destruction: Assessing the Risks*, OTA-ISC-559 (Washington, D.C.: U.S. Government Printing Office, August 1993), pp. 2, 46.

11. OTA, *Technologies Underlying Weapons of Mass Destruction*, p. 73.

12. U.S. Congress, Office of Technology Assessment (OTA), *Global Arms*

Trade: Commerce in Advanced Military Technology and Weapons, OTA-ISC-460 (Washington, D.C.: U.S. Government Printing Office, June 1991), ch. 1.

13. See National Academy of Sciences, National Research Council, *Balancing the National Interest: U.S. National Security Export Controls and Global Economic Competition* (Washington, D.C.: National Academy Press, 1987).

14. U.S. Department of Commerce, Trade Promotion Coordinating Committee, "The National Export Strategy: Annual Report to the United States Congress," October 1994, passim.

15. *Defense News,* February 20–26, 1995, p. 1.

16. For a discussion of this point see Leonard S. Spector, "Foreign-Supplied Combat Aircraft: Will They Drop the Third World Bomb?" *Journal of International Affairs* 40, no. 1 (Summer 1986): 143–57.

17. Stanford University, Center for International Security and Arms Control, *Assessing Ballistic Missile Proliferation and Its Control* (Stanford, Calif.: Stanford University Press, November 1991), pp. 25–26.

18. OTA, *Technologies Underlying Weapons of Mass Destruction,* p. 244.

19. White House, Office of the Press Secretary, "Conventional Arms Transfer Policy," Fact Sheet, February 17, 1995, p. 2.

20. *Washington Post,* April 12, 1995, pp. A1, A31.

21. The Pressler amendment is contained in subsection 620E(e) of the Foreign Assistance Act of 1961 (P.L. 87-195), which was added by section 902 of the International Security and Development Cooperation Act of 1985 (P.L. 99-83).

22. Senator Larry Pressler (R-S.D.), quoted in *Defense News,* April 3–9, 1995, p. 28.

23. *Washington Post,* April 8, 1995, p. A20.

24. It may be argued that advanced ICBM and long-range cruise missiles are just as effective as combat aircraft, but these are not widespread, especially in the developing world.

25. U.S. Congress, Office of Technology Assessment (OTA), "Civilian

Technology and Military Security," *Holding the Edge: Maintaining the Defense Technology Base*, OTA-ISC-420 (Washington, D.C.: U.S. Government Printing Office, March 1989), p. 176.

26. Jacques S. Gansler, *Affording Defense* (Cambridge, Mass.: MIT Press, 1993), pp. 273–82.

27. "To meet its technology needs, the Defense Department will be forced to rely increasingly on the commercial sector. Defense's shrinking share of Western world R&D cannot support a state-of-the-art military by itself. Defense will need to learn to draw on the larger, dynamic, and increasingly global commercial technology base." John A. Alic et al., *Beyond Spinoff: Military and Commercial Technologies in a Changing World* (Boston: Harvard Business School Press, 1992), p. 8.

28. Jonathan B. Tucker, "Lessons of Iraq's Biological Warfare Program," *Arms Control* 14, no. 3 (December 1993): 236–37.

29. Officers of the Merck Corporation, interview with author, names and date withheld.

30. OTA, *Proliferation of Weapons of Mass Destruction*, p. 6.

31. U.S. Congress, Office of Technology Assessment (OTA), *Proliferation and the Former Soviet Union*, OTA-ISS-605 (Washington, D.C.: U.S. Government Printing Office, September 1994), pp. 5, 29, 73. The United States took possession of 600 kilograms of highly enriched uranium from Kazakhstan in the fall of 1994, and has agreed to purchase 500 tons of highly enriched uranium from Russia over the next twenty years for $12 billion. *Washington Post*, June 25, 1995, p. A21.

32. See Kenneth N. Waltz, "The Spread of Nuclear Weapons: More May Be Better," *Adelphi Papers* 171 (1981): 1–32; John J. Weltman, "Managing Nuclear Multipolarity," *International Security* 6, no. 3 (Winter 1981/82): 182–94; and John J. Mearsheimer, "Back to the Future: Instability in Europe After the Cold War," *International Security* 15, no. 1 (Summer 1990): 5–56.

33. See, for example, Kenneth Waltz, *Theory of International Politics* (Reading, Mass.: Addison-Wesley, 1979), pp. 183–92.

34. Mearsheimer, "Back to the Future," 54.

35. John J. Mearsheimer, "Why We Will Soon Miss the Cold War," *Atlantic Monthly*, August 1990, pp. 35–42.
36. Waltz, "The Spread of Nuclear Weapons," 13.
37. Weltman, "Managing Nuclear Polarity," 187, 190.
38. U.S. Congress, Office of Technology Assessment (OTA), *Multinationals and the U.S. Technology Base*, OTA-ITE-612 (Washington, D.C.: U.S. Government Printing Office, September 1994), p. 106.
39. Some theorists argue that among advanced industrial states fundamental reinforcement for peace and stability comes from democratic forms of government. See, for example, Richard Doyle, "Liberalism and World Politics," *American Political Science Review* (December 1986). For a critique that favors the realist perspective, see Christopher Layne, "Kant or Cant: The Myth of Democratic Peace," *International Security* 19, no. 2 (Fall 1994): 5–49. The debate will continue, but is not central to the argument of this book.
40. *New York Times*, January 11, 1993, p. 1; *Washington Post*, March 31, 1993, p. A21.
41. U.S. Arms Control and Disarmament Agency, "Adherence to and Compliance with Arms Control Agreements and the President's Report to Congress on Soviet Noncompliance with Arms Control Agreements," January 14, 1993, pp. 15–16.

CHAPTER 3: AN AVALANCHE OF ARMS

1. According to intelligence analysts and video evidence, it is unlikely the Patriot succeeded in destroying any of the eighty modified Scud ballistic missiles fired from Iraq during the 1991 Gulf War. Israeli intelligence officials, interview with author, names and date withheld. See also George N. Lewis and Theodore A. Postal, "Video Evidence on the Effectiveness of Patriot during the 1991 Gulf War," *Science and Global Security* 4 (1993): 1–63.
2. DSAA officials in Washington, interviews with author, names and date withheld; and DSAA field officers in Japan, South Korea,

France, Germany, Belgium, Italy, and the United Kingdom, interviews with author, names and dates withheld.

3. As of September 1994, DSAA maintained approximately 857 personnel to staff its Security Assistance Organizations attached to the U.S. diplomatic missions in fifty-four countries. U.S. Department of State and U.S. Department of Defense, *Congressional Presentation for Promoting Peace* (Washington, D.C.: U.S. Department of State, 1995), pp. 195, 199.

4. U.S. Department of State, Office of Defense Relations and Security Assistance, "USG and U.S. Civilian Contract Personnel in Foreign Countries for Assignments in Implementation of Sales and Commercial Exports under the Arms Export Control Act," September 1994, table H, sec. 36(a)(7).

5. In FY 1993, the first year that an FMS cap was imposed by Congress, the FMS administrative account had a starting balance of $82 million, collected $503 million in fees, obligated $293 million, and had an ending balance of $292 million. Figures are from DSAA Memorandum for Mr. Todd Stein, Arms Control and Foreign Policy Caucus, U.S. Congress, "Subject: Congressman Skaggs' Request for FMS Administrative and Logistics Support Charge (LSC) Financial Activity," June 1994, p. 3.

6. Federation of American Scientists, *Arms Sales Monitor* 27 (November 30, 1994): 3; and State Department officials, interview with author, names and date withheld.

7. The 16 percent figure is the average, over ten years, of the difference between the dollar value of agreements and deliveries, divided by the dollar value of agreements for each year. With respect to ACDA data, the same figure is obtained by dividing the ten-year total of the difference between the dollar value of agreements and deliveries, by the total of the dollar value of agreements for the ten-year period. The different methods of calculation are used to compensate for the fact that U.S. Arms Control and Disarmament Agency (ACDA) data are presented in constant dollars and FMS data are in current dollars. See U.S. Arms Control and Disarmament Agency (ACDA), *World Military Expenditures and Arms*

Transfers 1990 (Washington, D.C.: U.S. Government Printing Office, November 1991), pp. 135, 140, for relevant data sets.

8. U.S. Department of State and U.S. Department of Defense, *Congressional Presentation for Promoting Peace*, 1995, pp. 189–90.

9. From U.S. Department of Defense, Office of the Undersecretary of Defense (Acquisition and Technology), *World-Wide Conventional Arms Trade (1994–2000): A Forecast and Analysis* (Washington, D.C.: U.S. Department of Defense, December 1994), p. 55. The $16-billion figure is expressed in 1993 constant dollars.

10. ACDA, *World Military Expenditures and Arms Transfers, 1991–1992* (Washington, D.C.: U.S. Government Printing Office, March 1994), p. 90; and ACDA, *World Military Expenditures and Arms Transfers, 1993–1994* (Washington, D.C.: U.S. Government Printing Office, February 1995), p. 98.

11. ACDA, *World Military Expenditures and Arms Transfers, 1991–1992*, p. 154.

12. "It should be noted that the arms transfer estimates for the most recent year, and to a lesser extent for several preceding years, tend to be understated. . . . In the U.S. case, commercial arms transfer licenses are now valid for three years, causing a delay in the reporting of deliveries made on them to statistical agencies." ACDA, *World Military Expenditures and Arms Transfers, 1991–1992*, p. 154.

13. U.S. Congress, Office of Technology Assessment (OTA), *Global Arms Trade*, OTA-ISC-460 (Washington, D.C.: U.S. Government Printing Office, June 1991), pp. 5–6.

14. *Washington Post*, September 20, 1990, pp. A1, A28.

15. *Congressional Record*, October 11, 1990, p. S14915.

16. House of Representatives, Committee on Foreign Affairs, Subcommittees on Arms Control, International Security and Science, and on Europe and the Middle East, *Proposed Sales to Saudi Arabia in Association with the Conduct of Operation Desert Storm*, 101st Cong., 2d sess., October 31, 1990, 42–687.

17. Quoted in Federation of American Scientists, *Arms Sales Monitor* 2 (April 1991): 1.

18. For Biden legislation, see S.1046, 102d Cong., 1st sess.; for hearings,

see U.S. Senate, Committee on Foreign Relations, Subcommittee on European Affairs, *America and Europe: Creating an Arms Suppliers' Cartel*, 102d Cong., 1st sess., April 23, 1991, 44–798.

19. *Washington Post*, May 30, 1991, p. 1; and *New York Times*, May 30, 1991, p. 1.

20. *New York Times*, May 30, 1991, p. 1.

21. U.S. Congress, Senate Committee on Foreign Relations, *Middle East Arms Transfer Policy*, S. Hrg. 102-245, June 6, 1991, 4.

22. Ibid., p. 32.

23. Ibid., pp. 26, 29.

24. Geoffrey Kemp, *The Control of the Middle East Arms Race* (Washington, D.C.: Carnegie Endowment for International Peace, 1991), pp. 15–16.

25. DSAA, *Foreign Military Sales, Foreign Military Construction Sales and Military Assistance Facts* (Washington, D.C.: FMS Control & Reports Division, Comptroller, DSAA, September 30, 1993), p. 3.

26. For details of the various legislative proposals see U.S. Congress, Congressional Research Service, *Weapons Nonproliferation Policy and Legislation*, CRS 91-536 F, July 3, 1991, updated August 30, 1991.

27. Présidence de la République, *Plan de maîtrise des armements et de désarmement* (Paris, June 3, 1991).

28. Andrew J. Pierre, "From Paris Comes Hope of Bold New Approaches," *International Herald Tribune*, July 17, 1991.

29. UN Security Council, Joint Communiqué, "Meeting of the Five on Arms Transfers and Non-Proliferation," Paris, July 8, 9, 1991.

30. U.S. Department of State, *Dispatch*, "Group of Seven (G-7) Summit Declarations," July 22, 1991, p. 526.

31. *Washington Post*, July 17, 1991, p. 1.

32. Arms exports are barred and specifically set forth under Export Trade Control Order of Japan and the Policy Guideline of the Government of Japan on Arms Export of February 27, 1976. The Japanese prohibition on the export of military technology has, however, been somewhat weakened by the increasing use of civil or dual-use technology in weapons systems. OTA, *Global Arms Trade*, pp. 109–11.

33. Japanese high-technology products are, however, incorporated into many foreign-made weapon systems. "It is generally conceded that it is nearly impossible to guard against the redirection of Japanese technology—especially basic or manufacturing technologies—to military purposes." Defense Budget Project, Memorandum from Richard A. Bitzinger to Members of the Senior Advisory Group, January 30, 1995, pp. 4–5.

34. Commonwealth Office, "Meeting of the Five on Arms Transfers and Non-Proliferation: London 17/18 October 1991," press release no. 172, October 18, 1991.

35. "Testimony of Ambassador Reginald Bartholomew, Undersecretary of State for International Security Affairs, Before the House Foreign Affairs Committee," text of statement, March 24, 1992, p. 3.

36. Abdul Aziz Said and Henry Kenny, "The Jericho Exchange: To Promote Peace, the U.S. Must Sacrifice the Profits of War," *Washington Post*, September 5, 1993, p. C1.

37. Only Russia retained the independent capability to produce a range of sophisticated conventional weapons. U.S. Central Intelligence Agency, Directorate of Intelligence, "The Defense Industries of the Newly Independent States of Eurasia," OSE 93-10001, January 1993, p. 1.

38. Foreign Broadcast Information Service, Analysis Report, "Russian Policy on Arms Sales," FB AR 92-10006, December 1, 1992, pp. i–iii.

39. *New York Times*, February 23, 1992, p. 1.

40. *Washington Post*, October 30, 1992, p. A29.

41. *New York Times*, October 18, 1990, p. A1.

42. *Washington Post*, December 19, 1992, p. A1.

43. Mr. William Grundmann, Director for Combat Support, Defense Intelligence Agency, Statement for the Record, U.S. Congress, Joint Economic Committee, June 11, 1993, p. 12.

44. Alfred B. Prados, "Middle East Arms Supply: Recent Control Initiatives," report, Congressional Research Service, IB91113, updated November 1, 1991, p. 8. Congress did, however, pass the the Foreign Relations Authorization Act, Fiscal Years 1992 and 1993, P.L. 102-138. Section 322 does contain language regarding

the transfer of defense articles to the Middle East, but it is far less detailed and less restrictive than related provision in H.R. 2508.

45. P.L. 102-138, section 322, October 28, 1991.

46. Congressman Howard L. Berman of the House Foreign Affairs Committee commented on the Bush decision to put the F-15 sale to the Saudis on a fast track and short-circuit the usual process for notifying arms sales to Congress: "Passing out 'goodies' in the election season to win votes is a tradition long honored by both Republicans and Democrats. But this time around, there are some big potential problems." *St. Louis Post Dispatch*, September 24, 1992, p. 22. In October, the U.S. president, vice president, and secretary of defense personally intervened to persuade the Kuwaiti royal family to buy 236 M1A2 Abrams tanks instead of British-made Challenger tanks. The price of the U.S. tanks and support package was set at $4 billion. General Dynamics argued that the Kuwaiti sale would help them save 5,900 jobs in Ohio and Michigan to the end of the decade. *New York Times*, October, 13, 1992, p. A1.

47. *Washington Post*, September 3, 1992, p. A12; September 4, 1992, p. A1.

48. *New York Times*, September 15, 1992, p. A1.

49. *Washington Post*, September 12, 1992; and Sharon Parnes, "F/A-18 Hornet Supplier Delegation Visits Israeli Firms," *Defense News*, March 9, 1992.

50. Brig.-Gen. Eytan Ben-Eliahu, quoted in *Defense News*, September 14–20, 1992, pp. 1, 50. The seventy-two aircraft, designated the F-15XP, are somewhat downgraded versions of the F-15E Strike Eagle; twenty-four have air-to-air interceptor capabilities, and forty-eight are equipped with navigation targeting pods which are integral to the ground attack capability.

51. The U.S. Defense Security Assistance Agency (DSAA), the agency responsible for carrying out the U.S. Foreign Military Sales (FMS) program, reported to the Congress that "the long term survival of a number of important domestic arms programs are tied to foreign sales: M1A1 Abrams battle tank, Blackhawk helicopter, HAWK surface-to-air missile, Boeing 707 aircraft, to name a few." U.S.

Department of State and U.S. Defense Security Assistance Agency, *Congressional Presentation for Security Assistance Programs*, fiscal year 1992, p. 6.

52. From brochures distributed by U.S. Jobs Now. U.S. Jobs Now is supported by a coalition of unions and defense companies including McDonnell Douglas Corporation, Pratt & Whitney, and Hughes Aircraft Company.

53. John C. Danforth, Richard A. Gephardt, William Clay, Christopher S. Bond, Joan Kelly Horn, and Harold L. Volkmer, Letter to President Bush, April 22, 1992.

54. "Britain Nails Down Gulf Sales: Saudi Arabia Buys 48 Tornados; Oman Opts for Challenger 2s," *Defense News*, February 1–7, 1993, p. 3.

55. *Washington Post*, October 17, 1992, p. A17.

56. DSAA, *Foreign Military Sales, Foreign Military Construction Sales and Military Assistance Facts*, pp. 52–53.

57. Cable from Acting Secretary Eagleburger for Ambassador/Charge on "Guidance Concerning Embassy Role in Support of U.S. Defense Exporters," unclassified version.

58. On the "defense GATT," see "The Future of Defense and Industrial Collaboration in NATO," a speech presented by Ambassador William Taft to the German Strategy Forum and the Institute for Foreign Policy Analysis in Bonn, Germany, March 15, 1990.

59. This would require the repeal of section 32 of the Arms Export Control Act of 1968. *New York Times*, March 18, 1991, pp. A1, D6.

60. *Washington Post*, May 8, 1992, p. 1.

61. For text of the president's address, see *New York Times*, March 7, 1991, p. A8.

62. Of that total, $16.6 billion was sold by the government through the Foreign Military Sales of the U.S. Defense Security Assistance Agency and $5.9 billion was sold directly by U.S. defense companies through commercial sales. *Congressional Record*, January 24, 1992, p. E-67. The detailed tabulation, placed in the *Congressional Record* by Representative Lee H. Hamilton, was provided to the Committee on Foreign Affairs on January 9, 1992, in a quarterly report in

compliance with section 36(a) of the Arms Export Control Act. The U.S. also forgave Egypt $8 billion in debt for arms previously transferred, and authorized Turkey to build and sell 50 F-16 fighters to Egypt as part of a deal to cut the Iraqi oil pipeline in Turkey.

63. U.S. Congress, Senate Committee on Foreign Relations, *Fiscal Year 1994 Foreign Assistance Authorization: Hearing before the Committee on Foreign Relations*, 103d Cong., 1st sess., May 5, 19, 27; June 16; and July 14, 1993, S. Hrg. 103-322, pp. 258–60.

64. Ibid.

65. "Conventional Arms Transfer Policy," Statement by the President, May 19, 1977, *Presidential Documents, Jimmy Carter*, vol. 13, no. 21, pp. 756–57. See also, Michael T. Klare, *American Arms Supermarket* (Austin: University of Texas Press, 1984), pp. 43–47.

66. Andrew J. Pierre, *The Global Politics of Arms Sales* (Princeton, N.J.: Princeton University Press, 1982), p. 65.

67. Ibid., pp. 58–59.

68. U.S. Department of Commerce, Trade Promotion Coordinating Committee, *The National Export Strategy: Annual Report to the United States Congress* (Washington, D.C.: U.S. Government Printing Office, October 1994), pp. 30–31.

69. U.S. Congress, House Committee on Foreign Affairs, *U.S. Policy on Conventional Arms Transfers*, 103d Cong., 1st sess., November 9, 1993, 74-781-CC, pp. 45–46.

70. Cited in ibid., p. 46.

71. Cited in *Arms Sales Monitor*, no. 26, July 30, 1994, p. 1. Original text in U.S. Congress, House Committee on Foreign Affairs, *U.S. Nonproliferation Policy: Hearing before the House Committee on Foreign Affairs* (Washington, D.C.: U.S. Government Printing Office, 1994), p. 80.

72. White House, Office of the Press Secretary, "Criteria for Decision-making on U.S. Arms Exports," Fact Sheet, February 17, 1995; and White House, Office of the Press Secretary, "Conventional Arms Transfer Policy," Fact Sheet, February 17, 1995.

73. William J. Perry, Memorandum for Secretaries of the Military

Departments, Chairman of the Joint Chiefs of Staff, Undersecretaries of Defense . . . , "Specifications & Standards—A New Way of Doing Business," June 29, 1994, p. 1.

CHAPTER 4: THE SPREAD OF MILITARY INDUSTRY

1. See William W. Keller, *The Liberals and J. Edgar Hoover: Rise and Fall of a Domestic Intelligence State* (Princeton, N.J.: Princeton University Press, 1989).
2. David J. Louscher and Anne Naylor Schwarz, "Patterns of Third World Military Technology Acquisition," in Kwang-Il Baek et al., eds., *The Dilemma of Third World Defense Industries: Supplier Control or Recipient Autonomy?* (Boulder, Colo.: Westview Press, 1989), p. 36.
3. Michael T. Klare, *American Arms Supermarket* (Austin: University of Texas Press, 1984), p. 168.
4. U.S. Congress, Office of Technology Assessment (OTA), *Arming Our Allies: Cooperation and Competition in Defense Technology*, OTA-ISC-449 (Washington, D.C.: U.S. Government Printing Office, 1990), p. 13.
5. From 1980 through 1987, the French sold $6.7 billion (current dollars) worth of advanced weapons to Iraq, including 143 Mirage F-1C fighters and 734 AM-39 Exocet missiles. U.S. Arms Control and Disarmament Agency (ACDA), *World Military Expenditures and Arms Transfers, 1988* (Washington, D.C.: U.S. Government Printing Office, 1989), p. 22.
6. These include the M1A1 Abrams tank, the Blackhawk helicopter, the HAWK surface-to-air missile, the F-16 fighter, the Apache attack helicopter, and the Boeing 707 aircraft, among others. Several of these were deployed effectively in the Persian Gulf War and were scheduled to go out of production as early as 1993. See U.S. Department of State and U.S. Defense Security Assistance Agency, *Congressional Presentation for Security Assistance Programs*, fiscal year 1992, p. 6.

7. Gregory W. Noble, *Flying Apart: Japanese-American Negotiations Over the FSX Fighter Plane* (Berkeley, Calif.: Institute for International Studies, 1992), pp. 11–12, 15.

8. Japanese military spending is technology intensive. In 1987, for example, Japan's defense budget was the sixth largest in the world, but Japan did not rank in the top twenty in terms of number of persons in its military services. ACDA, *World Military Expenditures, 1988*, p. 3.

9. Congressional concern is reflected in a report published one year later. See OTA, *Arming Our Allies*, p. 9.

10. United States General Accounting Office, *U.S.-Japan Codevelopment: Update of the FS-X Program*, GAO/NSIAD-92-165 (Washington, D.C.: U.S. General Accounting Office, 1992), pp. 4, 21.

11. Richard J. Samuels, *"Rich Nation, Strong Army": National Security and the Technology Transformation of Japan* (Ithaca, N.Y.: Cornell University Press, 1994), p. 2 and chap. 7.

12. Defense Science Board, *Defense Industrial Cooperation with Pacific Rim Nations*, (Washington, D.C.: Office of the Secretary of Defense, October 1989), p. viii.

13. For an analysis of defense production in Israel, South Korea, Brazil, India, Taiwan, Australia, Indonesia, and Singapore, see U.S. Congress, Office of Technology Assessment (OTA), *Global Arms Trade: Commerce in Advanced Military Technology and Weapons*, OTA-ISC-460 (Washington, D.C.: U.S. Government Printing Office, June 1991). See also, Carol Evans, "Defense Production in the NICs: The Case Studies from Brazil and India" (Ph.D. diss., London School of Economics, 1992).

14. Andrew L. Ross, "Full Circle: Conventional Proliferation, the International Arms Trade, and Third World Arms Exports," in Kwang-Il Baek et al., eds., *The Dilemma of Third World Defense Industries*, p. 30.

15. Ian Anthony, "The 'Third Tier' Countries: Production of Major Weapons," in Herbert Wulf, ed., *Arms Industry Limited* (Oxford, Eng.: Oxford University Press and Stockholm International Peace Research Institute [SIPRI], 1993), p. 365. The study quoted is

SIPRI, *The Arms Trade with the Third World* (Almquist and Wiksell: Stockholm, 1971), p. 782.

16. Anthony, "The 'Third Tier' Countries," p. 367.

17. See Herbert Wulf, "Developing Countries," in Nicole Ball and Milton Leitenberg, *The Structure of the Defense Industry* (New York: St. Martin's Press, 1983), p. 310.

18. For a comprehensive treatment of the U.S. military technology base, see U.S. Congress, Office of Technology Assessment (OTA), *Holding the Edge: Maintaining the Defense Technology Base*, OTA-ISC-420 (Washington, D.C.: U.S. Government Printing Office, April 1989).

19. For fiscal years 1994 and 1995 the RDT&E budget was $34.7 and $35.5 billion, respectively. U.S. Department of Defense, *Budget for Fiscal Years 1996 and 1997, RDT&E Programs (R-1)* (Washington, D.C.: U.S. Department of Defense, February 1995), p. II.

20. Theodore J. Lowi, *The End of Liberalism* (New York: Norton, 1979).

21. Louscher and Schwarz, "Patterns of Third World Military Technology Acquisition," p. 51.

22. "[The] most important element of the arms producing exporters' success has been their ability to acquire and absorb Northern technology, in the form of license agreements, technical data packages, technical training programs, joint research and development ventures, and even the provision of turn-key factories, has played a crucial role in the establishment and growth of the Third World's defense industries. By acquiring foreign technology, the Third World's arms producers have been able to build their defense industries on proven, standardized technology. Without the benefits of this near-massive transfer of military technology from North to South, few developing countries would no[w] be producing, much less exporting, arms." Ross, "Full Circle," pp. 19–20.

23. U.S. Congress, House Committee on Foreign Affairs, *U.S. Policy on Conventional Arms Transfers: Joint Hearing before the Subcommittees on International Security, International Organizations and Human Rights and International Operations*, 74-781-CC, 103d Cong., 1st sess., November 9, 1993, p. 10.

24. Officials at the McDonnell Douglas Company, interview with author, names and date withheld.

25. Ibid.

26. Stephanie G. Neuman, "International Stratification and Third World Military Industries," *International Organization* 38, no. 1 (Winter 1984): 167–97; and Keith Krause, *Arms and the State: Patterns of Military Production and Trade* (Cambridge, Eng.: Cambridge University Press, 1992), pp. 31, 153–81.

27. Neuman, "International Stratification," p. 167.

28. Neuman's count, based on her private data base, is lower than those of other authors who base their calculations on more public sources. According to one authority, "[b]y the early 1980s, 54 developing countries were manufacturing major military equipment, small arms, or ammunition. Thirty-six of the 54 were producing at least one of the four major types of conventional weapons. Seven countries—Argentina, Brazil, Egypt, India, Israel, South Africa, and Taiwan—had built up an across-the-board production capability by the early 1980s." Ross, "Full Circle," pp. 4–5. Other authors take direct issue with both Neuman's data and the accompanying arguments. See, for example, Anne Naylor Schwarz, "Arms Transfers and the Development of Second-Level Arms Industries," in David J. Louscher and Michael D. Salomone, eds., *Marketing Security Assistance: New Perspectives on Arms Sales* (Lexington, Mass.: Lexington Books, 1987), pp. 102–5.

29. Krause, *Arms and the State*, p. 31.

30. Ibid., pp. 153–55, 181.

31. Ian Anthony, *The Arms Trade and the Medium Powers: Case Studies of India and Pakistan 1947–1990* (New York and Hertfordshire, Eng.: Harvester Wheatsheaf, 1992), p. 181.

32. United Nations Conference on Trade and Development, Programme on Transnational Corporations, *World Investment Report 1993: Transnational Corporations and Integrated International Production* (New York: United Nations, 1993), p. 14, table I.1.

33. For a broad overview, see U.S. Congress, Office of Technology

Assessment (OTA), *Multinationals and the U.S. Technology Base,* OTA-ITE-612 (Washington, D.C.: U.S. Government Printing Office, September 1994).

34. The results of the Defense Budget Project study and a fuller analysis of these data can be found in Richard A. Bitzinger, "The Globalization of Arms Production: Defense Markets in Transition" (Washington, D.C.: Defense Budget Project, December 1993); and Richard A. Bitzinger, "The Globalization of Arms Industry: The Next Proliferation Challenge," *International Security* 19, no. 2 (Fall 1994).

35. Louscher and Schwarz, "Patterns of Third World Military Technology Acquisition," p. 51. The detailed findings of the study and the data on which they are based are found in David J. Louscher and Michael D. Salomone, *Technology Transfer and U.S. Security Assistance: The Impact of Licensed Production* (Boulder, Colo.: Westview Press, 1987).

36. Louscher and Salomone are aware of this problem and have expressed it in strong terms: "[L]icense and coproduction of major weapons seems to be fairly well monitored, but licenses to produce minor weapons systems or support systems are not as well monitored. Licenses to produce components are scarcely monitored. The epistemological problem here is that what is observed is real but what is not observed may also be real and of a greater magnitude than what is observed." Louscher and Salomone, *Technology Transfer,* p. 10.

37. European components alone accounted for 10 percent of the value of all F-16s bought by the United States Air Force. Robert H. Trice, "Transnational Industrial Cooperation in Defense Programs," in Ethan B. Kapstein, ed., *Global Arms Production: Policy Dilemmas for the 1990s* (Cambridge, Mass.: Center for International Affairs and University Press of America, 1992), p. 174.

38. OTA, *Global Arms Trade,* p. 8.

CHAPTER 5: POLITICS OF THE
GLOBAL ARMS ENTERPRISE

1. U.S. Congress, Office of Technology Assessment (OTA), *Building Future Security*, OTA-ISC-530 (Washington, D.C.: U.S. Government Printing Office, June 1992), p. 103. From *Washington Post*, March 9, 1991, p. C2. In 1995 Martin Marietta merged with the Lockheed Corporation, the world's largest arms company with a combined sales of $22.9 billion in 1994. Of that total, $3.9 billion (or 17 percent) was foreign sales. Company officials expected the percentage of foreign sales to grow in future years. Lockheed Martin officials, interview with author, names and date withheld.

2. On April 1, 1992, "Thomson-CSF, Hughes Aircraft Co. and the Carlyle Group offered to purchase the LTV Aerospace and Defense Group for $400 million. Thomson-CSF and Hughes Aircraft would pay $280 million in cash for the Missiles Division, while the Carlyle Group would pay $120 million ($90 million in cash and $30 million in preferred stock) for the Aircraft Division." LTV News Release, "Chronology Pertaining to the Sale of LTV Aerospace and Defense Activities," April 29, 1992, p. 3.

3. *Aviation Week & Space Technology*, April 20, 1992, p. 64.

4. Thomson-CSF, "Benefits of the Acquisition," internal document, April 3, 1992. A list of Thomson-CSF facilities in the U.S. appears on page 5.

5. "Statement of James D. Bell, Chairman and President, Thomson-CSF, Inc., before the Subcommittee on Defense Industry and Technology, Senate Committee on Armed Services," text of statement, April 30, 1992, p. 5.

6. LTV Aerospace and Defense Company, "Capabilities from the Ground Up," sales brochure, n.d, p. 7.

7. "Testimony of Norman R. Augustine, Chairman and Chief Executive Officer, Martin Marietta Corporation, before the Subcommittee on Defense Industry and Technology, Senate Armed Services Committee," text of statement, April 30, 1992, p. 27.

8. "Statement of John Gardner," January 16, 1992; quoted in *Defense News*, February 3, 1992.

9. "Statement of Frank C. Carlucci, Vice Chairman, The Carlyle Group, before the Subcommittee on Defense Industry and Technology, Senate Committee on Armed Services," text of statement, April 30, 1992, p. 5.

10. "Statement of Frank C. Carlucci, Vice Chairman, The Carlyle Group, before the Defense Policy Panel and Investigations Subcommittee, House Armed Services Committee," text of statement, May 14, 1992, p. 16.

11. "Testimony of Norman R. Augustine," p. 4.

12. Ibid.

13. From Martin Marietta Corporation, "Aerospace/Defense Industry Consolidation—1988–1992 Transactions," information provided to author, September 8, 1992. Acquisition list and tables provided by Martin Marietta Corporation from their study of defense industry acquisitions.

14. Ibid.

15. *Wall Street Journal*, September 2, 1992, p. 1.

16. Section 835 of the FY 1993 Defense Authorization Act prohibits foreign-controlled firms from acquiring U.S. defense companies that have been awarded contracts in excess of $500 million by the Energy or Defense Departments. In all, thirty-five U.S. defense firms were placed off-limits to foreign governments.

17. *Financial Times*, November 22, 1994, p. 1.

18. Deutch made his remarks at the Conference on Cutting Defense, Building Security, sponsored by the Medill School of Journalism and the John D. and Catherine T. MacArthur Foundation, Washington, D.C., February 22, 1994.

19. U.S. Congress, Office of Technology Assessment (OTA), *Holding the Edge: Maintaining the Defense Technology Base*, OTA-ISC-420 (Washington, D.C.: U.S. Government Printing Office, April 1989), p. 176.

20. Jacques S. Gansler, "Transforming the U.S. Defense Industrial Base," *Survival* 35, no. 4 (Winter 1993): 130.

21. See, for example, President's Blue Ribbon Commission on Defense Management, *A Quest for Excellence: Final Report to the President* (Washington, D.C.: President's Blue Ribbon Committee on Defense Management, June 1986).

22. See William J. Perry, "Specifications and Standards—A New Way of Doing Business," Memorandum for Secretaries of the Military Departments, Chairman of the Joint Chiefs of Staff, Undersecretaries of Defense . . . , June 29, 1994, passim.

23. *Washington Post*, Mar. 29, 1991, p. F1; *Wall Street Journal*, March 29, 1991, p. A3; *Defense News*, April 1, 1991, p. 4.

24. *Defense News*, September 12–18, 1994, p. 1.

25. John M. Deutch, "Department of Defense Conventional Arms Transfer Policy," Memorandum for Undersecretary of Defense (Policy), December 28, 1993, p. 2.

26. U.S. Congress, Office of Technology Assessment (OTA), *Lessons in Restructuring Defense Industry: The French Experience—Background Paper*, OTA-BP-ISC-96 (Washington, D.C.: U.S. Government Printing Office, June 1992), p. 8.

27. The inclusion of SM-39 antiship missiles, which can be fired while submerged, and air-independent propulsion (AIP), that enables diesel submarines to stay submerged for weeks, "will allow Pakistan to counteract the Indian Navy, which operates aircraft carriers and maritime strike aircraft." *Defense News*, September 26–October 2, 1994, p. 1.

28. Michael Brzoska and Peter Lock, eds., *Restructuring of Arms Production in Western Europe* (Oxford, Eng.: Oxford University Press and Stockholm International Peace Research Institute [SIPRI], 1992), p. 6.

29. Keith Krause, *Arms and the State: Patterns of Military Production and Trade* (Cambridge, Eng.: Cambridge University Press, 1992), p. 149.

30. Madelene Sandstrom and Christina Wilen, *A Changing European Defence Industry: The Trend Towards Internationalisation in the Defence Industry of Western Europe*, pamphlet (Sundyberg, Sweden: Swedish Defence Research Establishment, Department of

Defence Analysis, Institution of Defence Economy and Management, 1994), p. 74.

31. Brzoska and Lock, eds., *Restructuring of Arms Production in Western Europe*, p. 4.

32. Elisabeth Sköns, "Western Europe: Internationalization of the Arms Industry," in Herbert Wulf, ed., *Arms Industry Limited* (Oxford, Eng.: Oxford University Press and Stockholm International Peace Research Institute [SIPRI], 1993), pp. 168–88, tables 9.3–9.13.

33. Agnès Courades Allebeck, "The European Community: From the EC to the European Union," in Herbert Wulf, ed., *Arms Industry Limited* (Oxford, Eng.: Oxford University Press and Stockholm International Peace Research Institute [SIPRI], 1993), p. 191.

34. OTA, *Lessons in Restructuring Defense Industry*, p. 25.

35. Brzoska and Lock, eds., *Restructuring of Arms Production in Western Europe*, p. 10.

36. One of the strongest formulations of this view was given by Herbert Wulf as follows: "The arms industry in Europe is far from a unified industrial branch, and no multilateral institution in Europe has the authority to take procurement or industrial policy decisions. Arms-producing industries are constrained by national research and development and procurement budgets. Even in international collaborative projects, companies of a particular country can expect to receive a share of procurement orders that correlates highly to the financial burden which that country carries. Thus, the arms industry—although it is becoming increasingly internationalized—is still largely organized on a national scale." See Wulf, "Western Europe: Facing Over-Capacities," in Herbert Wulf, ed., *Arms Industry Limited* (Oxford, Eng.: Oxford University Press and Stockholm International Peace Research Institute [SIPRI], 1993), pp. 143–44, tables 9.3–9.13.

37. William Walker and Philip Gummett, "Nationalism, Internationalism and the European Defence Market," *Chaillot Papers* 9 (September 1993): 4.

38. *Air & Cosmos*, December 16, 1991, p. 6.

39. Foreign Broadcast Information Service, FBIS-WEU-94-165-S,

August 25, 1994, p. 1, based on a translation of a feature article by Jean-François Jacquier in the Paris industry weekly *L'Usine Nouvelle*, July 14.

40. Ethan B. Kapstein, "America's Arms-Trade Monopoly: Lagging Sales Will Starve Lesser Suppliers," *Foreign Affairs* (May–June 1994): 13.

41. *Defense News*, September 19–25, 1994, pp. 1, 44.

42. *Defense News*, November 21–27, 1994, p. 1.

43. Sandstrom and Wilen, *A Changing European Defence Industry*, p. 74.

44. U.S. Congress, Office of Technology Assessment (OTA), *Arming Our Allies: Cooperation and Competition in Defense Technology*, OTA-ISC-449 (Washington, D.C.: U.S. Government Printing Office, May 1990), p. 98.

45. U.S. Congress, Office of Technology Assessment (OTA), *Multinationals and the National Interest: Playing by Different Rules*, OTA-ITE-569 (Washington, D.C.: U.S. Government Printing Office, September 1993), pp. 1–2.

46. Barbara Wanner, "Washington Pushes for Expanded U.S.-Japan Defense Technology Exchanges," *JEI Reports* 14A (April 8, 1994): 3.

47. Department of Defense, "Technology for Technology (TFT) Initiative: New Opportunities for Defense Technology Cooperation between the United States and Japan," fact sheet, prepared by John L. Hopper/DUTP&IP/Far East/X54813/13, May 1994, pp. 1–2.

48. For a brilliant treatment of Japanese technonationalism, see Richard J. Samuals, *"Rich Nation, Strong Army": National Security and the Technological Transformation of Japan* (Ithaca, N.Y.: Cornell University Press, 1994).

49. Richard J. Samuels et al., *Defense Production and Industrial Development: The Case of Japanese Aircraft* (Cambridge, Mass.: MIT-Japan Science and Technology Program, 1988), p. 14.

50. See U.S. Department of Commerce, Bureau of Export Administration, Office of Industrial Resource Administration, Strategic Analysis Division, *National Security Assessment of the Domestic*

and Foreign Subcontractor Base: A Study of Three Navy Weapon Systems (Washington, D.C.: U.S. Government Printing Office, March 1992), pp. iv, 32.

CHAPTER 6: CONCLUSION

1. "Conventional Arms Transfer Policy," Statement by the President, May 19, 1977, *Presidential Documents, Jimmy Carter,* vol. 13, no. 21, pp. 756–57.
2. Leslie Gelb and other senior Carter appointees, interview with author.
3. Andrew J. Pierre, *The Global Politics of Arms Sales* (Princeton, N.J.: Princeton University Press, 1982), pp. 285–90.
4. Ibid., pp. 292–98.
5. William W. Keller, *The Liberals and J. Edgar Hoover: Rise and Fall of a Domestic Intelligence State* (Princeton, N.J.: Princeton University Press, 1989).

INDEX